# The American College and American Culture

# The American College and American Culture

## SOCIALIZATION AS A FUNCTION OF HIGHER EDUCATION

by *Oscar Handlin*

Director, Charles Warren Center for Studies in
American History, Harvard University

and *Mary F. Handlin*

An Essay Written for
*The Carnegie Commission on Higher Education*

MC GRAW-HILL BOOK COMPANY

New York   St. Louis   San Francisco   Düsseldorf
London   Sydney   Toronto   Mexico   Panama

*The Carnegie Commission on Higher Education,*
*1947 Center Street, Berkeley, California 94704,*
*has sponsored preparation of this essay as a*
*part of a continuing effort to present significant*
*information and issues for public discussion.*
*The views expressed are those of the authors.*

THE AMERICAN COLLEGE AND AMERICAN CULTURE
*Socialization as a Function of Higher Education*

Copyright © 1970 by The Carnegie Foundation for
the Advancement of Teaching. All rights reserved.
Printed in the United States of America.

Library of Congress catalog card number 79-118803

123456789MAMM79876543210

10015

# Foreword

Culture as a whole and higher education in particular have developed in more intimate contact with each other in America over the past three centuries than in almost any other nation. Higher education in the United States is marked by great diversity, yet there have been general tendencies in the evolution of all institutions. These tendencies have been deeply affected by the preoccupations and values of the nation and have been susceptible to continuous, often subtle, change.

Oscar and Mary Handlin have drawn on their deep knowledge of America to describe the shifting tides of public opinion and the responses by the colleges. They examine the functions of higher education that have changed less by written compact with society than by gradual amendment of tone and emphasis in response to society. The articulation of society and campuses in the United States has historically been close. Yet a time may now have come when the two are moving in quite opposite directions. This beautifully written essay provides an insightful background to the current crisis.

*Clark Kerr*

*Chairman*
*The Carnegie Commission*
*on Higher Education*

*May, 1970*

# Contents

# 1. A Statement of the Problem

The essay which follows traces the development of one strand in the general pattern of American higher education. The treatment is therefore necessarily somewhat out of focus. Factors other than those discussed here were always important; and, to some extent, to describe out of context one among the many forces which shaped the college in the United States is unavoidably to distort the whole pattern.

Yet there is a peculiar virtue to doing so. The aspect of higher education here analyzed has frequently been obscured. It has rarely entered into formal discussions of the philosophy of education and has been treated, if at all, as only incidental by both the critics and defenders of the colleges. Often, therefore, its significance in shaping the actual forms of higher education has been overlooked. The discussion which follows aims to clarify the history of the role of socialization as a factor in the development of the college in the United States.

**EARLY FORCES IN GROWTH** A variety of reasons entered into the formation of American colleges in the more than 300 years of their history. Consistently, from the earliest foundations to the most recent, a religious motive was present. This was not surprising in the societies in which the first colleges appeared. The Protestant emphasis on the learned ministry was particularly pronounced in the Puritan colonies, which ascribed a special importance to the proper intellectual discipline in the training of the clergy. The insistence upon that need contributed substantially to the impulse to form the first institutions of higher learning in this part of the New World.

The religious factor was more general, however. It included also a missionary element. Again and again Americans reminded themselves of the obligations to propagate the faith among the

1

aborigines, to further piety and safeguard doctrinal purity along the frontiers, and, ultimately, with the multiplication of sects, of the need of each to protect and spread its membership. All these objectives, it was argued, would be served by creating additional colleges under church auspices.

In addition, as in the European universities which were the progenitors of the American, there was also a professional motive for creating these institutions. The early colleges were not simply to inculcate religion, they were also to train ministers. Later, they acquired the additional tasks of preparing their graduates for the practice of law, medicine, and the variety of other callings which acquired professional status in the New World. Since it was always difficult in the United States to define or delimit professional privileges, the number of callings to which the college became the entry expanded rapidly.

Furthermore, the university was considered "useful" to the society which supported it, although the character of that presumed utility was rarely described with precision or clarity. The frequency with which the argument of usefulness was advanced was, no doubt, due to the low esteem in which most Americans held purely intellectual activities. The universities were always frail and underprivileged, lacking autonomous financial or social support. Often their promoters and administrators had to make a case for them on grounds other than those of the intrinsic merit of scholarship, and the plea consistently most persuasive was that of utility. The community that invested in a college would ultimately profit from it. It was rarely necessary to be more specific.

A similar claim, equally difficult to substantiate, was addressed to the individual. The university was a channel of social mobility. The youth who put in his time would gain a career advantage over his peer who did not. At what stage this factor became important is uncertain. Quite early on, it was apparent that bright young persons were being recruited for the clergy. Probably that practice had European antecedents. But by the eighteenth century, the university offered, or claimed to be, a channel for advancement in various other careers. The precise relationship of higher education to social advancement is by no means clear. It is doubtful that the university added very much in this respect down until practically the end of the nineteenth century. On the one hand, some students attended against the wishes of hardheaded parents who saw no use to the waste of time in idle study. On the other, some of the most ambitious and enterprising young men did not seek this particular means of advancement. Still, the belief in college as a means of social ascent was always a factor of some consequence, although its precise weight cannot be fully measured.

The concerns with religion, with professional training, and with the possibilities of mobility were genuine and were present through much of the history of higher education in the United States. But they do not exhaust the causes that entered into the formation and development of the university, which also served another purpose and was intended to do so. Young men — and later women — sought it out, parents paid its tuition, and the community contributed to its maintenance because it was regarded as a medium for education in a more general sense than that encompassed by its religious or professional purposes.

**THE SOCIALIZING FUNCTION** The nature of that more general purpose is the subject of the analysis which follows. There will be no attempt at this point to define that purpose except by postulating its existence apart from the other kinds of factors already enumerated. Since the conception embraced elements of drastic change as well as of remarkable continuity, an inclusive a priori definition would have to be qualified, conditioned, and modified as the discussion proceeded. It seems preferable to let the meaning of that nonreligious, nonvocational function emerge from the specific descriptions of it in each period.

This much can be said at the outset: Insofar as the education administered by the college was neither totally religious nor totally professional, it was connected with the desire to adjust the individual to the society within which he would play a part. That is, attendance at college was an aspect of his socialization. Precisely how the process of socialization operated depended not only on the college as an institution but also upon the changing structure of the society into which the individual would move and on the changing conception the individual held of himself.

These elements passed through radical alterations during the 300 years of development which are the subject of our concern. The first universities appeared in a colonial society that clung desperately to the edge of the wilderness, and they served a population which still conceived of the individual in Renaissance terms. The institutions established before 1770 were joined by many more in the next century. In that era, national self-consciousness and rapid expansion reshaped the character of American society

and also significantly influenced the personality types who suc-
ceeded within that society and whom the colleges would serve.

In the last third of the nineteenth century, the universities
changed drastically under the impact of shifts in the social order
connected with industrialization and also under the influence of
changes in the kind of people whose children went to college.

Finally, some four decades ago, a new period began which may
or may not already have come to a close. Its dominant social features were economic growth, war, and science. Its primary demand
upon the individual was the ability to work in large groups. These
social and personal changes were also involved in the way in which
the university evolved. Although it is too early to say whether this
period is really over, it provides the immediate background for
the problems which trouble the college today.

The account which follows must therefore trace the intersection of forces of a quite diverse nature—the university itself, the
society it serves, and the type of population drawn into it. Out of
that intersection came the evolving concept of the institution as a
force for socialization.

The peculiar nature of American development for long periods
obscured such terms as *college, university,* and *academy,* which
in other contexts had a clear and precise meaning. This analysis
will deal with institutions which granted the first, or bachelor's,
degree, however they may have been denominated at any given
moment. In the effort to do so, the analysis will encounter problems that arise both out of excessive inclusiveness and out of excessive exclusiveness. Because of the pluralism of nineteenth-cen-
tury American society, many different kinds of institutions will
have to be considered together. Yet the colleges will be discussed
apart from the academies with which, at least until the Civil War,
they had much in common. These problems are created by the data,
which as in so many features of the development of higher education, are far from neat. Only by recognizing that lack of neat-
ness and of precision of boundaries can the actuality of history
be described.

# 2. Colonial Seminaries, 1636–1770

In 1770, American higher education, measured from the founding of Harvard University, was already 134 years old. Yet relatively little had happened during this long period. In the first century-and-a-third of collegiate experience, the original institution in Cambridge had been joined by eight others: in Williamsburg, Virginia; in New Haven, Connecticut; in Princeton and New Brunswick, New Jersey; in New York City; in Hanover, New Hampshire; in Philadelphia, Pennsylvania; and in Providence, Rhode Island. All were small. Each struggled with difficulty to survive and each produced only a handful of graduates. Harvard in the seventeenth century usually managed to award degrees to four or five candidates a year (Morison, II, 1936a, p. 423). Its largest class was to come in 1771, and numbered 63. The newer institutions, such as Princeton and Pennsylvania, were smaller. In 1770, the total living alumni of all the colleges were fewer than 3,000.[1]

The rather minor role of the university was not surprising. Even the ancient European seats of learning were small in size and served but a tiny fraction of the population. It was hardly to be expected that their counterparts would be greater in the New World, where men's main preoccupation was survival. The important tasks in America were the establishment of settlements, the advance upon the frontier, and the development of a viable economy. Comparatively little energy went to education at any level, and only a handful of young men went on to college. The wilderness was not a setting conducive to the development of studious personalities. Childhood ended early and adulthood followed immediately. Young men struck out for themselves as soon as they were physically able to do so, for challenging opportunities existed everywhere. It

[1] McAnear, 1955, p. 24ff.; Vinton, 1878, pp. 102, 103; Stillé, 1878, p. 129; Morison, 1936b, p. 102; Eells, 1958, p. 36.

is less surprising that there were so few graduates under these conditions than that there were any at all.

Small, weak, and uninfluential as they were, the colleges nevertheless passed through a significant phase of development in the colonial era. In the seventeenth and eighteenth centuries American higher education established institutional roots important for the future, and it then already displayed characteristic traits that would persist for a long time thereafter.

**PURITANISM AND LEARNING**

Colonial colleges were the rather unexpected products of a peculiar combination of causes. They were far from being simply replications of English or European models. They took form out of the conditions of migration and settlement.

The establishment of colleges in the Colonies was not as natural for Englishmen as "to dress for dinner in the jungle" (Rudolph, 1962, p. 4). Such institutions had appeared in Spanish America, where they served the needs both of the Catholic religious orders which administered them and of a highly developed and wealthy society which afforded its uppermost groups abundant leisure. The same needs did not exist in the English possessions, where there was no established corps of teachers and where the primitive communities were barely capable of sustaining themselves. Furthermore, higher education was not a usual feature of English colonies in other parts of the world (Kingsley, 1878, p. 68ff.; Clark, 1889, p. 25ff.). The universities of the mother country had places enough for the scions of colonial families. Young men from the American mainland had no difficulties in securing admission to Oxford, Cambridge, Dublin, or Edinburgh. There was something anomalous about the sprouting colleges of New England, Virginia, and the middle colonies.

Puritanism was certainly a factor. One of the first things the Massachusetts settlers "longed for, and looked after, was to advance *Learning* and perpetuate it to Posterity" *(New England's First Fruits,* 1643, pp. 12–14). This unusual group of migrants included more than 100 graduates of Cambridge and Oxford. The faith that had led them across the ocean also animated the desire to make some provision that would assure the colony of a continuous supply of learned ministers.

Yet Puritan piety need not in itself have led to the establishment of a university in America. It would have been simpler to send promising young men for their training to Cambridge, which had nurtured so many leaders of the Bay Colony. Puritans were in control in England after 1640 and had enough influence to purge its universities of Papist doctrines and of other unwholesome influences.

The Massachusetts Puritans, however, wanted a college of their own. Their mission in the New World was to create a city upon a hill that would light the way to redemption for all mankind; and they considered Harvard a necessary ornament of their commonwealth. Once established it had to be sustained in order to prove the validity of the New World experiment as well as to produce proper ministers (Johnson, 1910, p. 61).

The Harvard experience was symptomatic of a general desire to use higher education as a means towards religious ends. Again and again, the missionary impulse led to the formation of colleges to train ministers, to convert the Indians, and to sustain the faith of people remote from the centers of civilization. These motives were explicit in the establishment of William and Mary and of Dartmouth, and, heightened by the prevailing sectarianism of the eighteenth century, they were influential in the history of Yale, Princeton, Queens, and the College of Rhode Island (Stillé, 1878, pp. 122, 123).

Yet bound in with these expectations of what the college could do was another, somewhat vaguer, motive. Despite all the rhetoric about the value of learning, the colonists showed little solicitude for education at the levels at which it might have affected substantial numbers of people (Bailyn, 1960, p. 27ff.). If there was more concern over colleges than over common schools, it was not because the former met an existing need, but because of their symbolic importance and because of the prestige they brought to the communities in which they were situated. The prolonged battle between Wethersfield and New Haven over the possession of Yale was the first of frequent assertions of the influence of local pride (Kingsley, 1878, p. 66ff.). But pride, prestige, and symbols did not bear a high cash value in the Colonies, with the result that the institutions, so hopefully founded, never enjoyed adequate means of support. Financial deprivation exerted a significant effect on their future development.

**THE QUEST FOR FUNDS** The fact that the colleges satisfied an ideal aspiration rather than an actual social demand prevented them from conforming to English precedent as their founders intended them to, and also pressed novel functions upon them.

Emmanuel College of Cambridge and Queens College of Oxford,

graduates of which were prominent among the colonists, were the models for the first American institutions of higher education. Yet striking differences soon appeared in type of students, finances, government, and instruction.

American society lacked the gentry class, which in England sent its sons to the university and also provided the means of its support. The colonial families with aristocratic pretensions, such as the Byrds and Delanceys, were few in number and, if they were interested in higher education, were as likely as not to ship their boys off to the mother country (Stillé, 1878, p. 125). The American colleges were by no means egalitarian; they gave ample recognition to social distinctions. Family status, along with other factors, influenced the order in class at Harvard and was also deferred to elsewhere (Shipton, 1954, p. 258ff.; Morison, II, 1936a, p. 452). Nevertheless, there never appeared the separation accepted at Oxford and Cambridge between gentlemen and commoners or between earned and pass degrees. The intention may have been present; social realities did not permit its implementation.

University resources therefore remained meager. Virginia took steps to establish a college in 1619 and again in 1660 but did not celebrate a commencement until 1700. Yale received its charter in 1701 but took almost two decades to get into operation. South Carolina could not realize its ambitions at all in this period (Meriwether, 1889, p. 52). President Chauncy of Harvard complained in the 1660s of the wealthy who waxed fat, yet refused to support learning. A century later, President Witherspoon of Princeton might well have echoed these sentiments as he appealed to pulpits throughout the colonies in the effort to extinguish the college debt (Morison, I, 1936a, p. 330; Vinton, 1878, p. 102). There were few generous donors; £550 was so extraordinary a gift that Elihu Yale, who made it, was immortalized in the name of the college which benefited from it. He, like the other great benefactors of these years, was an Englishman rather than a colonial. In recognition of the fact that donors were more numerous across the Atlantic, emissaries from Pennsylvania and New York in 1762 canvassed the mother country for contributions to their colleges. In any case, there were no stable channels for investing whatever endowment was received, so that the institutions were always dependent on current income to meet current expenses (Stillé, 1878, p. 129; Bailyn, 1960, p. 42).

The hard-pressed college authorities often appealed for support to local and provincial governments, which sometimes responded with cash for a building, sometimes with the grant of a privilege — to operate a ferry, to conduct a lottery, or to secure the proceeds of special taxes. But there was nothing munificent about the sums thus made available. That was why the suggestion in 1762 that Massachusetts might charter a college in Hampshire County threw Harvard into a panic. Competition, a committee of the Board of Overseers explained, would weaken the two institutions, cheapen the value of the degree, and set back the cause of education in general. What the committee really meant was that there simply was not enough in the provincial coffers to go around (Quincy, II, 1840, p. 106ff.; Bush, 1891, p. 62).

In the last analysis, the universities depended for survival on student fees. Beacons of learning though they might be, the flame would flicker out unless their administrators could persuade young men and their parents that education was worth payment of the price. To do so, the colleges had to assume functions only tangentially related to the purposes stated in their charters.

**THE VALUE OF THE DEGREE** The reasons for seeking a college degree varied. In some callings, the completion of the course was a distinct help, even when it was not an absolute condition of access. The Quakers, who objected to a hireling ministry, and the New Lights and Baptists, who valued the conversion experience over formal education, did not look to the universities for their leaders. But the degree was essential to the young man who aspired to a place in a solid, established church (Morison, 1936b, p. 86).

About half the graduates of seventeenth-century Harvard entered the ministry. But already in 1647 President Dunster expressed the hope of encouraging scholars who would go on to practice all the professions; and in the first hundred years of the institution, a substantial number of alumni became physicians and schoolmasters, and some went on to be merchants or simply gentlemen. There were even a few lawyers. In the eighteenth century the proportion of college men who went on to careers outside the ministry undoubtedly grew larger (Morison, 1935, p. 249; II, 1936a, pp. 562, 563).

Entry to none of those vocations depended upon possession of a degree, as the careers of John Marshall and John Rutledge demonstrated. Aspiring young men acquired the skill and earned the right to practice medicine, law, or trade through apprenticeship, and that situation persisted well into the nineteenth century. Fifteen-year-old John Adams did not come to Harvard for purely professional reasons. Ambitious, he wished to rise above the humble circumstances of his parents, and the law was to be the means by which he would do so. However, the prerequisite to admission to the bar was a period of reading and service, not in college but in a lawyer's office.

For young men like Adams, the value of a higher education lay not in professional training but elsewhere. It derived from the belief that the course of learning endowed those who completed it with cultural attributes that were signs of superior status. This was by no means a crude, calculating attitude, but rather one composed of multiple, scarcely conscious, sets of values. The ability to quote a Greek maxim in a legal brief was not essential but helpful. More important was the prevailing conviction that those who had sharpened their minds on the complexities of Greek thought would be better able as a result to deal with the day-to-day problems of trespass and contract. Most important was the awareness that colonial society still put a premium on and assigned practical rewards to people who could display such signs of gentlemanly rank as command of the classics.

The concept that there was an "order of learning apt for a gentleman" had originated in the Renaissance and had been elaborated in England by Sir Thomas Elyot, who argued also that mastery of that order ought to precede the study of medicine or law. Proposals in the late sixteenth century to create special academies for young English noblemen proved fruitless, for the universities had already assumed the task of providing oversight for the youth of the gentry (Woodward, 1967, pp. 280, 296).

Although counterparts of the English gentry were rare in the New World, the American universities increasingly edged toward a concept of education which involved training in proper behavior, unrelated to vocational goals. As was appropriate to seminaries, the chief purpose of which was the preparation of ministers, the emphasis was at first moral. President Dunster thus directed his tutors to do what they could to advance learning, but "especially to take care" that the students' "conduct and manners be honorable and without blame" (Morison, I, 1936a, p. 19). The William and Mary charter of 1693 advanced as justifications for the new institution not only the training it would offer potential clergymen but also its services in assuring youth a pious education "in good Letters and Manners" (Godbold, 1944, p. 5).

In the eighteenth century the gentlemanly ideal was somewhat more clearly set off from the old moralistic injunctions. The charter of the College of Rhode Island (1764) explained, "Institutions for liberal Education are highly beneficial to Society, by forming the rising Generation to Virtue Knowledge & useful Literature & thus preserving in the Community a Succession of Men duly qualify'd for discharging the Offices of Life with usefulness and reputation" (Bronson, 1914, p. 1; Thwing, 1906, p. 105ff.). At somewhat the same time, Provost William Smith in Philadelphia was arguing that "Thinking, Writing and Acting well" were "the grand aim of a liberal education." The college, he urged, was "to lay such a general foundation in all the branches of literature, as may enable youth to perfect themselves in those particular parts, to which their business or genius, may afterwards lead them" (Cheyney, 1940, p. 83; Stillé, 1878, p. 124; Doolittle, 1878, p. 152).

Liberal education, training in proper manners of action and thought, had a clear — though not always perceived — link with gentlemanly ideals. The connection emerged in the fear expressed by one friend of universities lest learning "become cheap and too common" so that "every man would be for giving his son an education" (Easterby, 1935, p. 10). It was also perceived by a hostile critic, young Benjamin Franklin, who, in *The New England Courant,* accused Harvard of being a refuge of wealthy young men, "where, for want of a suitable Genius, they learn little more than how to carry themselves handsomely, and enter a Room genteely" (Morison, 1936b, p. 61).

**THE DISCIPLINE OF YOUTH**  There was a very thin line between the desire of parents to send their sons off for a liberal education and the desire to subject unruly youngsters to control they were not receiving at home. The line was soon crossed. For centuries, the practice of western European families had recognized the advantages of subjecting youth to a firmer discipline than their own fathers would provide. Apprenticeship was the most common form of that practice in the American Colonies, for it combined training in behavior with training in a craft. Attendance at college became the variant for some people with aspirations above those of the artisans. When the conditions of life in the Colonies eased, a growing, though small, number of families could afford to provide their sons with an interval of study between childhood and adulthood.

No sooner was Harvard established than embarrassed parents perceived its potential as an asylum for 14- or 15-year-old sons who were idle, disobedient, or too much interested in plantation sports. By 1651, there were complaints against men who presumed "to send their most exorbitant children" to the Cambridge institution (Morison, 1935, p. 171; I, 1936a, pp. 77–78). Yet the inclination to do so increased with the passage of time and, in the eighteenth century, was a significant element in the recruitment of students.

It was not surprising therefore that discipline sometimes seemed to be the main business of the college. President Eaton, wrote William Hubbard (class of 1642), was "fitter to have been an officer in the inquisition, or master of an house of correction, than an instructor of Christian youth" (Morison, 1935, p. 228). Often he had to be! Compulsory attendance at chapel, fixed schedules of daily life, regulations about dress, common meals, and strict oversight of conduct and of pastimes were among the methods of inculcating proper habits of behavior. Frequent appeals to piety sought to bring religious sanctions to bear upon the young, for the colleges were still in 1770 essentially clerical institutions. When these means of persuasion did not suffice, the teachers could resort to floggings—at Harvard at least to 1718—or to boxing the ears of offenders. Moreover, the pattern of college life was designed to have the same effect. For instance, the custom that freshmen fagged, or ran errands for their seniors, gave a majority of the students an interest in conformity and generated a desire in those who suffered in their first year to impose the same system upon their successors in the next three (Morison, II, 1936a, pp. 417, 452ff.; Quincy, I, 1840, pp. 440, 442; II, pp. 91, 96ff.; Vinton, 1878, p. 101).

There is evidence enough that some disciplinary measures were necessary; the behavior of the collegians was far from exemplary. At the opening of the eighteenth century a Harvard tutor warned his charges to beware of drinking and card playing which "make the Colledge stink" (Morison, II, 1936a, pp. 456, 462). Again and again, the lads had to be punished for intoxication and carousing; for shooting or stealing turkeys, geese, and other fowl; for the atrocious crime of committing fornication; and for other varieties of abominable lasciviousness. However pure the college might be, corruptions in the environment were contagious. Massachusetts law forbade innkeepers and others to entertain scholars, but enterprising young men had no difficulty in securing access to adequate supplies of rum and girls. The students were difficult to control, for they knew that in town the lads and wenches met to drink and dance and were altogether brazen about it. One of them in 1676–77 had reminded his elders that if there was a war to be fought, "it must be the young men that must do it" and threatened "to burne the towne over their eares" if his personal life were interfered with (Morison, II, 1936a, pp. 459, 461). No wonder that the frequenting of ale houses, breaches of the Sabbath, and pranks in which windows were broken were common. Sometimes disobedience flared out into unrestrained riots, the best-known of which was the Harvard food rebellion of 1766 (Quincy, I, 1840, p. 443; II, pp. 90ff., 96ff.; Bush, 1891, p. 57ff.).

As far back as 1656, Harvard had appealed to the civil authorities to deal with the "unruly college boys," for there was no doubt that college criminals should fare no better "or otherwise than similar offenders outside Parnassus." Administrators were quick to condemn unlawful combinations of students "to force an execution of the laws of the college in such a manner as they think proper," and they had the support of public opinion "in their endeavors to restore and maintain a due subordination in the society."

There was nevertheless an inclination toward indulgence, for outbreaks of violence seemed characteristic of the history of universities since the Middle Ages. In the nature of the case, punishment for lesser offenses than rebellion was not severe—occasional blows from a tutor, fines, admonishment, and, only as a last resort, expulsion. Even those dismissed generally could earn forgiveness by public confession and a promise of better behavior in the future (Morison II, 1936a, p. 461ff.; Bush, 1891, pp. 28ff., 59). In part the willingness to pardon offenders was due to the tolerance of teachers reluctant to damage the careers of their charges. But it also sprang from parental pressure, as when a father objected to having his son at Harvard flogged like a beast (Morison, 1936b, p. 113). Such pressure was potent, for it was the parent who paid the fees upon which the colleges depended. Harvard in 1749 was destitute enough to be willing to alter the mode of commencement in return for a gift from three fathers of seniors (Quincy, II, 1840, p. 92ff.). Two decades later, the same institution readmitted some of the rioters it had expelled because friends and benefactors "condescended to intercede in their behalf" (Quincy, II, 1840, p. 118). Pressure from parents, at about the same time, was one of the factors that forced President Clap to resign from Yale (Kingsley, 1878, p. 72ff.).

**COLLEGE ORGANIZATION** The realities of dealing with a heterogeneous, and only partly interested, student body had more effect upon college life than idealistic aspirations toward learning. It was no doubt a desire to be quit of these disciplinary responsibilities, or at least to reduce their weight, that lay behind Increase Mather's recommendation to the founders of Yale that they have their students board in town under the guardianship of worthy families. But the burden was not so readily displaced; parents wished the college to bear it (Morison, II, 1936a, pp. 499–500).

The recruitment of faculty under these circumstances was, at best, a haphazard and difficult process. With rare exceptions, such as Henry Flynt, who remained 40 years at Harvard, the tutors were recent graduates who spent a few years in service before moving on to more desirable posts. Since their tasks were primarily disciplinary, vigorous young men, close in experience and physical strength to their charges, were likely to be most effective. It was also helpful that they be bachelors so that they could live on the premises. They were of course expected to conform to the religious views of the colleges and were in trouble if they did not. As a result, these were not particularly desirable jobs, and Yale on one occasion found itself without any staff at all (Vinton, 1878, p. 100; Kingsley, 1878, p. 73ff.).

By contrast, the position of president, which had no precise English model, was important. The office had continuity, prestige, and some degree of power. In most places there were no professors with fixed educational functions or salaries. Sometimes, indeed, the president was the only teacher. Always he was the source of discipline, the continuing force in setting instructional policy, and the focus of the authority to dispose of the college's financial resources. It was an indication of the weight attached to that position that Princeton was willing to send to Scotland for a man competent to fill it (Vinton, 1878, p. 101).

The curious etymological change which obliterated the distinction between university and college also reflected the special conditions of the colonial institutions. In England the university was the degree-granting, examining, instructional body, within which colleges housed communities of students and masters. In the colonies, there was persistent confusion over these terms, which in the end came to be used synonymously—an indication of the lack of clarity of objectives in institutions which had somewhat incongruously joined degree-granting academic attributes to quasi-parental supervisory functions.

**THE CURRICULUM**   The hazy goals of the colonial colleges created an unending set of dilemmas for their administrators. Founded for grandiloquent motives and inflated by community pride, these institutions never-theless staggered along in abject poverty. Dedicated to grand as-pirations for the pursuit of learning, they devoted much of their energy to the discipline of unruly boys. Above all, they lived under the shadow of day-to-day dependence upon fees and gifts that drove them to repeated exercises in self-justification.

The effect was uncertainty of purpose, visible in the curriculum — to some extent in changes in what was actually taught, but to a much greater extent in the rhetoric about what should or might be taught.

The seventeenth-century Harvard course of study, modeled upon that of the old Cambridge, had focused upon the languages — Latin, Greek, and Hebrew — presumably helpful to future ministers. Stu-dents whose destination was not the pulpit were expected to adapt themselves to the same basic requirements, since they were not in college to acquire any specific body of knowledge, but for a more liberal purpose — to learn to think like scholars and to behave like gentlemen.

The impetus toward change came from the enthusiasm of the rare teachers who felt the desire to convey their knowledge to any prospects and, even more, from the need of the colleges to justify themselves to potential donors and to fee-paying parents.

The eighteenth-century colleges could not remain altogether immune to the Enlightenment which was transforming the world of the intellect outside them. Occasional instructors began to draw upon the new ideas, both because of their attractiveness and be-cause arousing interest in some subject was one way of maintaining student discipline. Thomas Clap's public lectures at Yale and President Witherspoon's course in "mental science" at Princeton were among the innovations of this sort (Kingsley, 1878, p. 69ff.; Vinton, 1878, p. 101ff.).

**THE ARGU-MENT OF UTILITY** The curriculum also reflected the pressure from the lack of reliable sources of income. The colleges were forced to seek support from the community, failing which they could make ends meet only from student payments. The religious justification for appeals for funds persisted through the eighteenth century but lost some of its power when the Great Awakening increased the number of sectarian institutions competing for the limited resources available (Quincy, II, 1840, p. 40ff.).

Promoters and administrators were then tempted to fall back upon the argument that higher education was a service to the state and thus lend plausibility to their appeals to parsimonious colonial legislatures. The argument was familiar and had been consciously advanced from the time that a royal grant had established King's College in old Cambridge (Cobban, 1969). The friends of the new Cambridge in the 1660s supported appeals for funds with the reminder that the college had supplied the province with educated gentlemen for the magistracy. A decade later, a commencement orator explained that without the university, Massachusetts would have been "overwhelmed by lewd fellows of the baser sort" and its laws made by "plebiscites, appeals to base passions, and revolutionary rumblings" (Morison, 1935, pp. 228, 249, 250). The charter to Yale expressed the hope that the college would fit youth to public employment in the "civil state" as well as in the church; and there was a proposal in 1724 to convert William and Mary into a school for civil servants. Similar aspirations crept into statements at the founding of Columbia and Princeton (Thwing, 1906, pp. 67, 116; Adams, 1887, p. 21; Wertenbaker, 1946, p. 16ff.). Perhaps the most sweeping endorsement came from the pen of George III in an appeal for support of the colonial colleges in 1762. These seminaries, he pointed out, guarded a population drawn from different parts of the world against ignorance and instilled into it "a Love of Our excellent Constitution" (Van Amringe et al, 1904, p. 32).

The argument was, however, double-edged. Some legislators, listening to a commencement orator deplore the influence on the populace of mad nobodies and haranguers at street-corners, snapped shut their purses. Members of the assemblies who had themselves never been to college were reluctant to vote public funds to support would-be gentlemen who, the word had it, dressed in gold or silver lace, brocades, and silk nightgowns. The reluctance grew stronger in the eighteenth century, when habits of deference to the gentry faded (Morison, II, 1936a, p. 443; Bush, 1891, p. 58n.).

Hard-fisted farmers, calculating merchants, even aggressive, expansive planters were more likely to respond to a somewhat different justification: the college deserved support because of its utility. President Clap of Yale in the 1760s thus explained that graduates of that institution had "applied the principles of mechanical and experimental philosophy to the improvement of Agriculture, and have been able to instruct their neighbors in the science, for the publick Good" (Thwing, 1906, p. 105). The claim to usefulness was rarely made that precise and was often acknowledged to be more potential than actual. Yet the willingness to subject the college to the test of that criterion left the college vulnerable to pressures it could not resist.

William Penn had long before worried about the useless aspects of education, which left uncultivated and neglected men's "natural genius to mechanical, and physical or natural knowledge" (Woody, 1923, p. 8ff.). The concern, often reiterated, raised a troubling question: Were the classical languages and the rest of the inherited curriculum really relevant to the lives of the students subjected to them?

The effort to answer exposed the colleges to ceaseless discussion of innovations for which the claim of utility could be made. John Winthrop at Harvard and Ezra Stiles at Yale introduced instruction in science; and in Philadelphia William Smith, with Franklin's aid, put the emphasis on English, science, and practical studies rather than on the classics, although insisting that the students each day "converse with some one of the ancients who at the same time that he charms with all the beauties of his language is generally illustrating that particular branch of philosophy or science to which the other hours of the day are devoted." Yet it was after those changes had been made that John Trumbull, tutor at Yale, in a poem entitled "Progress of Dullness," attacked the existing curriculum for its neglect of literature (Cheyney, 1940, pp. 71–83; Stillé, 1878, p. 123ff.; Kingsley, 1878, pp. 69–72, 75).

The criterion of practical usefulness was not an effective guide to organization of the course of instruction. Apart from those destined for the ministry, the students had no clear idea of why they were in college; and prospective merchants, lawyers, and landowners were no more easily persuaded of the future utility of French and chemistry than of Greek and logic. Raising the issue led to vague promotional promises that could not be fulfilled. King's (Columbia) College thus announced that it would teach "every Thing *useful* for the Comfort, the Convenience and Elegance of Life," along with information about "the chief *Manufactures* relating to any of these Things" and also the knowledge of God and man that would contribute to true happiness (Snow, 1907, p. 57). The expectations thus nurtured exposed the colleges to demands that they teach whatever any influential group considered useful. Thus Pennsylvania in 1765 acquired a medical faculty without forethought and without consideration of its place in the college.

The arguments of service to the state and of utility, raised before 1770, were to acquire additional importance thereafter. They reflected the anomalous condition of the college in American life. The pride that entered into the foundation of seminaries of learning in the New World was not enough to sustain them for their own sake. To survive, they had to provide a gentlemanly liberal education to young men in the awkward age between childhood and independence. The colleges were far from having solved the problem of what that schooling should be when the Revolution created a new situation in the society of which they were a part.

# 3. Republican Culture, 1770–1870

The century after 1770 saw some fundamental changes in the American colleges. Most visible was the vast increase in the number of institutions and of students. By 1870, some 500 institutions were awarding bachelor's degrees to aspiring scholars—a total larger than that in all of Europe. Almost as dramatic was the apparent multiplication in the types of institutions. The old colleges became private corporations. These were joined by a variety of newer sectarian institutions, each with objectives peculiar to its particular founders, and by state universities. Both the mushrooming numbers and the diversity seemed simply to reflect the educational needs of society in a period marked by a spectacular growth of population which spread swiftly across the whole continent (Rudolph, 1962, p. 44ff.).

There is a measure, but only a measure, of truth in this commonly accepted explanation. Analysis of the connection between the social milieu and the proliferation of colleges will show that the multiplication of these institutions was not simply in response to demand. Growth was rather a reaction to complex impulses and it raised serious questions, then, as in the future, about the function of the university.

**THE EFFECTS OF THE REVOLUTION** The social context within which higher education developed in the century after 1770 was the product of the American Revolution, of the situation of youth in an expanding economy, and of the persistent pluralism of American religion. The interaction of these forces had a direct effect upon the colleges of the United States.

The implications of the Revolution for higher education were subtle—stimulating, yet paradoxically enervating. In the new independent Republic a learned magistracy and an informed populace seemed to some citizens more important than ever before. A bill to reform William and Mary in 1779 explained that the semi-nary was now to endow with science and virtue those who were to be the future guardians of the rights and liberties of their country. Jefferson envisaged the university as the capstone of a complete educational system which would train each man for a role in society appropriate to his ability. There was a general hope that the schools, at little cost, would "bring every section of the community in harmonious relations" and provide a lasting guaranty of unity and freedom (Bruce, I, 1920, pp. 48ff., 51ff.; Meriwether, 1889, p. 140).

The belief that education advanced the prosperity of society added another dimension to the argument in behalf of colleges. In time, that belief would find support in the link, established by educators, between economic development and "the intellectual improvement of a people." The government of a republic which abjured despotic or mercantilist methods could excite men to exer-tion and direct them to profitable ends by establishing colleges and furnishing them with "all the means for instruction, investi-gation and discovery" (Wayland, 1837, pp. 132–135; Meriwether, 1889, p. 134).

American nationalism, which was both a cause and a product of the Revolution, also influenced higher education. The Republic would justify itself in culture as well as in politics: it would pro-duce great universities as well as great literature and great art. Ohio and Georgia were not the only states with faith that they would be seats of the Athens of the future. A more realistic, though equally unfulfilled, expectation induced George Washington to leave part of his estate for the establishment of a national univer-sity. Dependence on Europe was so irksome and degrading that a Georgia legislature felt justified in penalizing students who at-tended foreign institutions. The New World would create new, unique, and superior colleges of its own (Richardson, I, 1896, p. 202; Candler, XIX, Part II, 1911, p. 378; Schmidt, 1930, p. 23ff.).

Finally, the democratic implications of the Revolution also stim-ulated university development. Independence, and then later the Jeffersonian and Jacksonian movements, diffused political power and reinforced the existing hostility to privilege or even to tokens of exclusive status. Opportunities were to be available to all, in education as in enterprise. If magistrates were to be educated, and if any man was inherently capable of becoming a magistrate, then all men were entitled to the opportunity of becoming educated. Anyone who wished to do so was therefore to be able to attend a college. Part of the design of Oberlin was "the education of the *common people* with the higher classes in such a manner as suits the nature of republican institutions." At Kenyon there were hopes of teaching the children of the poor to become schoolmasters, they in turn to help others rise by "merit into stations hitherto occupied by the rich" (Fairchild, 1878, pp. 326, 333; Smythe, 1924, p. 43; Havighurst, 1958, p. 45).

On the other hand, adjustment to the pressures generated by the Revolution was in some respects enervating. Nationalism sometimes hid a boastful provincialism and a parochial resentment of European connections that the new nation could ill afford in view of its own limited intellectual resources. All too often rhetoric became a substitute for performance. Furthermore, democracy created problems for institutions with pretensions to training an elite group, problems generally evaded by the assumption that anyone who willed it could be a member of such a group. The result was a consistent undervaluation of qualitative personal differences. There followed the drastic conclusion: If anyone ought to be able to go to college, then college ought to be such that it could teach everyone. Conscientious administrators could insist that colleges were "founded and endowed for the common good, and not for the private advantage of those who resort to them for education," from which it should have followed that the privilege of attendance would be available only to those qualified to use it toward the general welfare. But the argument was no more persuasive then than later. Nor did it shape admission policy (Hatch, 1927, p. 19).

**EXPANSION AND YOUTH** Expansion further complicated the contradictory impulses emanating from the national and democratic features of the Revolution. The growth of population and of the economy, the advance along the frontier, the constant founding of new cities and the development of new trade routes created tremendously exciting openings for youth. In the 1820s it was therefore perfectly feasible for an ambitious and able young man to rise to the command of a ship by the age of 20 and to have earned a fortune in a few years more. Moreover, the loosening of institutional restraints upon entry into the trades and professions enormously widened opportunities. Popular hostility to monopolies, privileges, and licenses of every sort put the right to practice law, medicine, or the ministry within the reach of many who had only perfunctory or informal training (Wayland, I, 1867, pp. 37, 53; Callcott, 1966, p. 105; Ames, 1878,

p. 43). In many careers, it was more and more often possible to abbreviate or completely to bypass the irksome apprenticeship of the past, so that an enterprising man could expect to make his mark quickly in any walk of life. Somewhat sadly Charles W. Eliot noted in 1869 that Americans were accustomed "to seeing men leap from farm or shop to court-room or pulpit" and "half believe that common men can safely use the seven league boots of genius" *(Addresses, Inauguration of Eliot,* 1869, p. 39).

College training might be useful in some callings, but it was also a postponement of the business of getting ahead. Now and again, a farm boy in homespun clothing and cowhide shoes, driven by some inner vision of the worth of learning, wandered into college and lived for four years on corn meal mush and sorghum to earn the degree. But more usually, active, vigorous young men— Jackson, Lincoln, Carnegie, Rockefeller—invested their time in the world, not in the classroom; and the popular accounts of success before 1870 rarely mentioned the utility of higher education. Nor did the lack of degrees or even expulsion hinder the advancement of Thomas Hart Benton or Abel P. Upshur or Andrew H. Holmes. Those eager to hasten along "the many avenues of wealth" which the commercial spirit of the country opened would not pause for intellectual accomplishments. While gaining knowledge, they would lose the opportunities to gain money. The clamor for admission by hordes of ambitious youths was not responsible for the multiplication of institutions.[1]

More commonly, the lads who went to college were those who looked forward to the burdens of manhood with some dread. "I was afraid to be a man," wrote one of them. "I was afraid to assume its responsibilities, and thought that I did not have sense enough to go out into the rough world, making a living as other men had to do. I was small in stature, and I did not feel that I had intellect enough to grapple with or to pit myself against such opposition as I should encounter in life." Such youths were likely to be aimless and haphazard in the choice of a career (Sims, 1885, p. 118; Wells, 1878, p. 190). Colleges, which grew in number for other reasons, offered many families an interlude for indecision. In a society which did not take it for granted that sons would follow the careers or reside in the communities of their fathers, choices were difficult and sometimes involved extended periods of uncertainty and con-

[1] Millis, 1927, p. 250ff.; Tappan, 1951, p. 64; Bush, 1891, p. 113ff.; Chambers, 1956, p. 16; "The Great Rebellion," 1907, p. 119ff.

flict. The college was a refuge where with communal approbation young men could separate themselves from their fathers and begin to chart independent courses through life.

The expectations of parents and children often diverged. The father of Abijah Whiting was dismayed to discover his son's change of prospective career from the ministry to law, a profession he doubted was congenial "to the practice of Personal Religion" and one about which "it has been much disputed of late years whether it is really beneficial to Society." On the other hand, the father of Marion Sims deplored the choice of medicine, a profession for which he had "the utmost contempt." Bemoaning the prospect that his son "should be going around from house to house through this country, with a pill box in one hand and a squirt in the other," he exclaimed, "There is no science in it. There is no honor to be achieved in it; no reputation to be made" (Pomfret, 1932, pp. 144–146; Sims, 1885, p. 116). But the old men had lost control.

A perceptive foreign observer perceived the extent to which democratic institutions weakened traditional parental authority. "As soon as the young American approaches manhood, the ties of filial obedience are relaxed day by day; master of his thoughts, he is soon master of his conduct. In America there is strictly speaking, no adolescence: at the close of boyhood the man appears and begins to trace out his own path." Tocqueville, however, did not fully understand the subtlety of the conflict between sons and fathers. It was true that "the same habits, the same principles, which impel the one to assert his independence predispose the other to consider the use of that independence as an incontestable right." Fathers, proud of their sons' abilities to find their own ways, were unwilling to erect restraining barriers that might limit the direction youth would take. Yet the hope persisted that the next generation would arrive at a destination approved by its predecessor. And the influence or discipline the parent could not or would not exert, might prove acceptable to young men if associated with the development of their own power and the rise in their own prospects for improvement (Tocqueville, II, 1944, p. 202).

President Francis Wayland of Brown described the process by which college separated the generations. The father sacrificed much to prepare his son for manhood. "It matters not how hard the parent may toil; he bears it patiently, that so he may render the life of his child less irksome. It matters not how neglected may have been the education of the father; he will see to it that the education of his son be not neglected." Poor families pushed forward children of talent so that "the son and brother may wear clothes such as they do not wear, eat from a table such as they do not spread, devote himself to quiet study while they are exhausted with toil, and enter upon a sphere of professional eminence where they know that they can never follow him" (Wayland, I, 1867, pp. 278, 281; Ticknor, 1825, p. 3).

The expectation was that college, which offered a gentlemanly upbringing as well as a liberal education, would endow its graduates with a general style of life rather than with a specific career. There was "no place so safe as a good college during the critical passage from boyhood to manhood," Charles W. Eliot insisted *(Addresses, Inauguration of Eliot,* p. 44). The Notre Dame catalogue of 1863 candidly explained that students would gain even if they learned nothing "but to converse and behave with the dignity and propriety of gentelmen" (Erbacher, 1931, p. 105; Porter, 1870, pp. 177-178). It was to aid in the acquisition of such graces that fathers responded to letters from their sons that "cried give, give, and said that money answered all things." The experience of the University of Marlyand illustrated the power of the aristocratic ideal. Its founders started with the intention of educating the rural masses to be "cheerful and happy under a sense of their peculiar advantages." By the time the institution opened five years later, it attracted not tillers of the soil but the sons of the well-to-do; and the catalogue promised to make its students "liberally educated gentlemen," developing in each "an aristocratic *corpora sana* through spartan discipline and outdoor exercise" (Pomfret, 1932, p. 138; Callcott, 1966, pp. 59, 60, 136-138, 147).

If some educators sensed a discrepancy between the code of the gentleman and democratic aspirations, they quieted their uneasiness with the reflection that anyone in the Republic could become a man of distinction through education. At the very time that they sought a wide student body, colleges also did all they could to keep alive the consciousness of their aristocratic antecedents and elite characteristics. Even the best established of these institutions were eager to demonstrate that their degrees were not "mere baubles" and hastened to enroll among their alumni, *honoris causa,* wandering noblemen, popular authors, indeed anyone whose name attracted public attention ("Glimpses of Old College Life," 1900, p. 158; Cometti, 1969, pp. 91-92, 116; Morison, 1936b, p. 187).

In the last analysis the esteem accorded the degree was the advantage of the college over the academy. Both institutions assumed the task of disciplining young men with whom the family could not cope at home. Francis Scott Key conceded in 1827 that no father could oversee his son's "morals, direct his judgment, restrain his passions, and guide his pursuits with the same advantages as a well-conducted college." President Wayland of Brown recalled parents without number who informed him of the peculiarities of sons entering as freshmen, "stating that their dispositions were excellent if they were only governed in some particular manner." Of course, he soon learned that "these *peculiar* young men were in fact, in almost every case, spoiled children" who would make more than the usual trouble (Wayland, I, 1867, p. 262; Callcott, 1966, p. 60; Fleming, 1936, p. 47). The place for them was in the growing number of academies and military schools—or in a college, which had the additional prestige of the degree it could award and the polish it could bestow (Sims, 1885, pp. 54ff., 71).

**THE PROLIF-ERATION OF COLLEGES** The pervasive sectarianism of American religious life remained after 1770, as before that date, the most common source of the impulse to found a new college. Each sect wished to train its own ministers, hold the loyalty of its own young people, and convert outsiders; it was plausible to imagine that an institution of higher education would serve all those purposes, especially along the advancing frontier. The fever affected such groups as the Baptists, Methodists, and Universalists, who had not earlier valued an educated ministry highly. Denominational competition undermined the calm assurance with which Asbury once wrote, "The Lord called not the Methodists to build colleges." In the nineteenth century they had to keep up with the other sects. And even when the initial exaggerated expectations subsided, the founders continued to hope that they could at least exclude dangerous doctrines and provide a "Christian," if not a sectarian, education. Scores of little campuses survived in expression of that hope; still more failed to survive.[2]

Local pride often sustained the religious impulse. Every fledgling community envisioned itself a distinguished future seat of learning, not merely out of the inevitable boosterism of the times, but also

[2] Winchester, 1878, p. 304; Sweet, 1937, p. 26; Sears, 1922, p. 35; Tewksbury, 1932; Schmidt, 1930, p. 19ff.; Power, 1958, pp. 41, 42; Doolittle, 1878, p. 153ff.; Hitchcock, 1863, pp. 56, 177–178; Bush, 1891, p. 271ff.; Rudolph, 1962, p. 35.

because colleges, like prisons, asylums, and other public institutions, contributed to the economic growth of the town—or so it was believed. The value of real estate would rise, and the professors and students who were purely consumers would bring outside money into communities always short of cash. Political pressure thus forced South Carolina in the 1790s to establish five colleges in various parts of the state, all stillborn or sickly. Many towns encouraged their academies to blossom into colleges, a transformation certainly flattering to headmasters who thereupon became presidents (Meriwether, 1889, pp. 52ff., 133; Bush, 1891, pp. 225, 251–257; Millis, 1927, pp. 33ff., 96ff.).

Local promoters got behind every project of a collegiate character. Although a bachelor's degree was not required for admission, the medical college established in Maryland in 1807 five years later determined to turn itself into a full-scale university. Tulane University took a somewhat similar course. When the American Literary, Scientific, and Military Academy in 1829 moved under a cloud to Norwich, Vermont to become a university, the site it abandoned in Middletown, Connecticut was put to use by the founders of Wesleyan.[3]

Nothing stopped the increase in numbers. Some critics pointed out that it would have been more advantageous to build secondary schools to prepare students adequately for the existing colleges. But the same hostility to privilege that made college attendance a right also put the charter within the reach of any applicant. The foes who sought to prevent the establishment of Amherst and Trinity quickly discovered that every group was as free to found a university as to found a bank or any other corporation. Furthermore, the pervasive federalism of the American political system encouraged the diffusion of institutions of higher education. Congress never did provide for a national university, but beginning with the Northwest Ordinance of 1787, it consistently appropriated lands in aid of state activities.[4]

The limits on the expansive capacity of the old established colleges also inhibited any inclination to restrain the growth in the number of new ones. The techniques for accommodating more than a few hundred students in a single institution were not then avail-

[3] Callcott, 1966, p. 16ff.; Dyer, 1966, pp. 18–22; Winchester, 1878, p. 303; Morison, 1936b, p. 336ff.

[4] Morgan, 1933, p. 22; Adams, 1878, p. 342; Rudolph, 1962, p. 51ff.; Handlin, 1961, p. 96.

able, nor was the capital needed to erect the buildings. And the logistic problems of housing and managing larger cohorts would not be solved until well after the Civil War. Colleges multiplied freely without effective opposition from those already in existence.

The increase in numbers was not, however, a measure of prosperity. Many colleges never existed except on the paper on which their charters were printed. Others got their start slowly and painfully. The University of Alabama, created in 1820, inaugurated its first president in 1831; Maryland, originally incorporated in 1807, awarded its first undergraduate degree in 1859. Of those which did actually come into being, only a minority were able to survive; and those which escaped extinction staggered from one financial expedient to another. Low budgets were characteristic; $6,000 for a whole year was a sizable sum. To draw in extra cash, some institutions added preparatory departments, and one even rented its classrooms to ice cream vendors and clubs. Colleges kept going because their faculties were willing to accept low salaries and menial extra tasks. "An indolent teacher will soon degenerate into a very stupid man," was President Wayland's rather smug justification for the incredible burdens of the teaching staff.[5]

Long after the Revolution the colleges continued to lack resources for much the same reasons as before 1770. Endowments were pathetically low; the University of Pennsylvania, for instance, added not a dollar to its total in more than 80 years. In 1862, Hanover College had an endowment of about $122,000 which, however, included $36,000 in unproductive real estate, $46,000 in unpaid pledges, and $34,000 already consumed for current expenses. Furthermore, in the absence of reliable channels of investment, the little stores of capital brought meager returns and were periodically diluted by inflation. Gifts were few and small: the $50,000 Abbott Lawrence gave Harvard was considered unusually generous; $10,000 in 1865 was enough to set Princeton to building an observatory; and Colonel Henry Rutgers in 1825 had a university named for him for half that sum. Some institutions began to organize their alumni in the 1820s. But those former students who became ministers were rarely in a position to make contributions, and more opulent graduates preferred to dispose of their benefac-

[5] Wayland, I, 1867, p. 235; Clark, 1889, p. 31ff.; Tewksbury, 1932, p. 28; Callcott, 1966, pp. 30, 54, 58; Meriwether, 1889, p. 134; Bush, 1891, p. 258ff.; Dyer, 1966, pp. 26, 28; Brocklesby, 1878, p. 265; Millis, 1927, pp. 20ff., 114ff.

tions otherwise. Wayland bitterly criticized the diversion of funds to missionaries who "carried absurd dogmas to the Burmans, who had a plentiful supply of their own. Had the same pains been taken at home to remove poverty, ignorance of natural laws, to abolish slavery, drunkenness, and prostitution and to teach piety and morality in general, what a good result would have come from it."[6]

The colleges continued unhappily and hazardously to depend on current income from students. Yet tuition charges reduced the number of applicants, since only the very wealthiest families escaped entirely the necessity of thinking of costs. The marginal value of the luxury supplied, the large number of competing purveyors, and violent fluctuations in the size of the clientele forced the colleges to operate in an uncertain market. Enrollments tended to decline in periods of prosperity, when opportunities elsewhere attracted young men; and rises in tuition were not feasible during depressions, when more students appeared. Earnest, needy young men then commonly interrupted their studies to replenish their resources by teaching school. Often the students who drifted in and out on a part-time or intermittent basis outnumbered those in the regular course. The sale of perpetual scholarships, which exempted all members of a family from future tuition charges in return for a single down payment, was self-defeating. Rutgers, which resorted to the expedient after 1850, desperately lowered the price from $500 to $100, to no avail. Since admission came at the very start of the school year, and transfers from one institution to another were easy and frequent, administrators never knew in advance the size of enrollments or of incomes and always had to budget parsimoniously. When the number of students fell, salary cuts hit not only the faculty but even the president.[7]

**JUSTIFYING COLLEGE EDUCATION** Unremitting financial stringency forced the colleges into an endless routine of self-justification. Only thus could they attract gifts from individual donors, from denominational sponsors or from the state; and only through persuasive proofs of usefulness could they draw a

[6] Wayland, II, 1867, p. 117; Millis, 1927, p. 123; Vinton, 1878, p. 112; Stillé, 1878, p. 132; Doolittle, 1878, p. 157; Brocklesby, 1878, pp. 265, 267; Winchester, 1878, pp. 306, 310; Adams, 1878, p. 345; Durfee, 1860, p. 196ff.

[7] Wayland, I, 1867, p. 209; Pomfret, 1932, pp. 140, 144, 146; Curti & Carstensen, I, 1949, p. 185; Callcott, 1966, p. 58. There has been no systematic study of the subject, but there are fragmentary data in college histories, e.g., Morison, 1936b, pp. 253, 317, 365; Winchester, 1878, p. 306; Clark, 1889, pp. 42, 53, 84, 102; Vinton, 1878, p. 106; Doolittle, 1878, p. 159; March, 1878, p. 286ff.

steady flow of fee-paying students. The pressure toward self-justification was the common condition that imposed a considerable degree of uniformity on all these institutions, despite the variety of impulses that entered into their establishment (Kingsley, 1878, p. 77; Bush, 1891, pp. 83, 225–226; Wells, 1878, p. 187).

In the scrabble for customers, the colleges competed not only with one another but also with the academies. Where a minimum admission age was fixed at all, it was usually 14, and there were always exceptions that were considerably lower as well as considerably higher (Schmidt, 1930, p. 78; Bush, 1891, p. 110; Power, 1958, p. 61). Parents ready to send their sons away had to be convinced that the college was a worthwhile alternative, or supplement, to the academy. For some, the degree itself seemed to have value. But the piety of a president capable of maintaining moral standards, the learning of an eminent faculty, and the utility of the course of study were also important in attracting students and in commanding community support.

The college president was still almost invariably a clergyman. The professor of mathematics appointed to that post at Yale in 1817 prudently was ordained the day he took office. Religious administration still seemed valuable, although the training of ministers had long since ceased to be the primary function of the college (Kingsley, 1878, p. 83; Dyer, 1966, p. 25).

The faculties varied enormously in character and in quality. The absence of formal qualifications for appointment and the low salaries produced haphazard and diversified staffs. But already in the eighteenth century, and increasingly thereafter, the teachers showed a preference for specialization by subject and for lecturing instead of recitations, changes, it was argued, which relieved the dullness of a classroom in which the student was expected to be "a pretty good reciter" of what he "understood dimly, or not at all." And, indeed, in the recollections of alumni, lectures—no matter what the subject—seem to have been the most valuable features of their studies (Wayland, I, 1867, p. 32ff.; Bush, 1891, p. 190).

As the means became available, the colleges demonstrated their excellence by appointing professors of natural philosophy, of divinity, of oratory, or of exact science. But rarely could the holders of those chairs indulge in genuine specialization. Princeton brought the distinguished chemist John Maclean from Glasgow, but asked him also to teach mathematics, natural history, and natural philosophy. Benjamin Silliman was about to enter the practice of law when he was appointed to a chair at Yale and, after two years of study, began to lecture on chemistry, mineralogy, and geology. The founder of American mineralogy taught mathematics and philosophy at Bowdoin; and such combinations as rhetoric, logic, theology, philosophy and political economy were not unusual in an instructional load (Vinton, 1878, p. 105; Kingsley, 1878, p. 80ff.; Packard, 1878, p. 198ff.).

To attune the contents of instruction to the capabilities and interests of the faculty and students demanded a departure from the old curriculum. The classics were an easy target; preoccupation with them disqualified young men for "the rugged realities of life" since "the most important knowledge or thought of our race" was to be found outside the writings of the ancient heathens. Nor did many institutions insist on the primacy of the formal study of divinity; even Amherst, founded for the "classical education of indigent young men of piety and talents for the Christian ministry," nicely obscured its intentions with the assurance that it would provide instruction "in all the branches of literature and science usually taught in colleges." It was therefore not difficult to substitute French for Greek or Moral Philosophy for Evidences of Christianity. But to combine the diverse elements into a seemingly planned whole that would be attractive to parents, meaningful to boys both admitted and graduated according to lax requirements, and within the competence of the available teachers was a far more difficult matter. It was not uncommon, after a spurt of reform, to revert to the tried and true staples for want of genuine alternatives.[8]

Caprice and accident played too large a role in the development of the chairs, departments, and faculties of many institutions to permit an overall view of their educational task. Oberlin, for instance, acquired its theological school as a result of a secession of abolitionists from Lane Seminary and derived its music department from the talent of a single student. Concerned trustees helped shape the curriculum at South Carolina. And Cousin's report on Prussian education influenced the state superintendent of education and through him the University of Michigan.[9]

[8] Meriwether, 1889, pp. 139, 141; Wayland, II, 1867, p. 86; Hitchcock, 1863, p. 160ff.; Bush, 1891, pp. 151, 191, 225ff.; Fairchild, 1878, p. 329; Porter, 1870, pp. 11ff., 14; March, 1878, p. 283ff.; Clark, 1889, p. 49; Rudolph, 1962, pp. 42, 43.

[9] Fairchild, 1878, p. 331; Meriwether, 1889, p. 137ff.; Adams, 1878, pp. 343, 345; Bush, 1891, pp. 109, 166; Kingsley, 1878, p. 82ff.; Brocklesby, 1878, p. 268ff.

It was tempting to seek a solution in the elective principle: the professors could teach what they wished, and the students would choose freely among the offerings set before them. The change would only extend to degree candidates the liberty that many colleges all along were according part-time scholars, the so-called special students. But President Jared Sparks of Harvard reported after a brief trial that while the elective system was "attractive in theory," it "never fulfilled all the expectations of its framers, and it soon began to fall into partial disfavor" (Bush, 1891, p. 167ff.; Bruce, I, 1920, p. 323ff.; Brocklesby, 1878, p. 270ff.).

Educators could not quite escape the dilemma involved in framing a curriculum by asserting that the object of the college was "not so much the accumulation of knowledge as the discipline of the mind." According to such an assertion it did not really matter what subject matter was presented to the students so long as their brains were exercised through precise analysis and open discussion. No doubt, a skillful and devoted teacher using that approach could make learning a memorable experience (Wayland, I, 1867, pp. 225, 233ff.; Schmidt, 1930, p. 112ff.). But the college lost some of its uniqueness if it offered its clients no more than a course of mental calisthenics; and so long as it continued to argue that there was a distinctive value to what it taught, it could not evade the responsibility of defining the specific subject matter.

An appropriate subject matter was at hand, science, and it commanded immense and growing prestige. Yet it was not readily adaptable to the actualities of American college life.

From the Enlightenment onward, in America as in Europe, there was a steady shift away from traditional to scientific knowledge, from faith in authority to a reliance upon rationality. The change in the ways of knowing was particularly significant in the United States, where the weakness of tradition had long nurtured habits of empiricism. It was not implausible to imagine, as some scholars did, that the university would become the seat of the new learning. When Americans began to reestablish connections with Europe after 1815, the institutions they visited or at which they studied in France and Germany certainly seemed worth emulating.

But the obstacles were formidable. For one thing, the belief in the value of experience and common sense retained extraordinary vitality. Benjamin Franklin was but the first of a succession of autodidacts who seemed to prove the superiority of a worldly to a cloistered life. An economist in 1833 deplored the fact that, by contrast with Europe, "the elementary truths" of his science were still a "matter of dispute in the Congress." He was not alone among scholars to be surprised by the American unwillingness to concede the validity of academic knowledge (Meriwether, 1889, p. 149; Richardson & Clark, 1878, p. 118; Doolittle, 1878, pp. 157–159).

Furthermore the universities, dependent on public and sectarian support, were slow to develop an association with science that might expose students to unconventional ideas. The infidel Thomas Cooper of South Carolina entertained the boys annually with a lecture challenging the authenticity of the Pentateuch. No one took "Old Coot" seriously or wanted to increase the number of like-minded teachers. President Josiah Quincy of Harvard in 1840 bravely announced: "The duty of considering science and learning as an independent interest of the community, begins to be very generally felt and acknowledged." But it was a feeble beginning in his day and gained little strength in the next three decades. In 1870, the academic environment was still far from congenial to science (Sims, 1885, pp. 82, 83; Morison, 1936b, p. 256; Meriwether, 1889, p. 150).

Men interested in the advancement of science did not conceive that the college was a likely setting for its pursuit. In the eighteenth century, they thought rather of detached learned societies and as late as Smithson's days continued to do so. Or if, like Jefferson, they did imagine that a university could find a place for scholarship, they thought of one unencumbered by undergraduates (Bruce, I, 1920, p. 332).

The few ambitious presidents like Philip Lindsley of the University of Nashville who wished to outdo the German institutions in scholarship and at the same time offer instruction to farmers and mechanics, proved utterly unrealistic. George Ticknor's blunt question of 1825 — "Who has been taught anything at our colleges with the thoroughness that will enable him to go safely and directly onward to distinction" in any department — remained dismayingly to the point almost a half-century later (Ticknor, 1825, p. 45).

The inability to give science or scholarship a central place in the curriculum was demonstrated by the unhappy fate of Harvard's effort to create "The Scientific School of the University at Cambridge" and to develop it into "an institution closely resembling the universities of Europe, especially those of Germany." The faculty which had proposed the scheme in 1846 had reasoned that "many students left college so young that they could, with great benefit to themselves, devote a year or two more to advanced studies," specializing in any one of the branches of learning, literary as well as scientific. "The teachers were ready, but," alas, "the students did not present themselves." Within a few years, the school was giving elementary practical instruction in some physical sciences, especially chemistry. It thus repeated the experience of the University of the City of New York (1830) whose ambitious plans for a scholarly institution faded into an inglorious compromise—a practical scientific course along with, and generally considered inferior to, the usual classical one. The same pattern emerged at Columbia, Yale, Dartmouth, and elsewhere (Ames, 1878, pp. 21-24; Adams, 1878, p. 347; Winchester, 1878, p. 307ff.).

Scientific courses faded into practical ones because the guidelines of college curricula were set not by the development of scholarship, but rather by the need to attract students and to elicit public or private support. On both accounts it seemed advisable to stress the utility of course offerings.

Declining enrollments in the 1840s made the need for change critical. President Wayland opposed a reduction in tuition which would touch off intercollegiate competition and result in "giving education away." Instead he called for "an honest, thorough, and candid revision" of a system too long shaped by authority and precedent. Shocked by a visit to Oxford—"too rich, too close a borough, and too much interested in the social system of England, to do anything valuable for the cause of science"—he concluded that Americans had copied Europe "without considering how entirely unsuited to our condition must be institutions founded for the education of the mediaeval clergy and modified by the pressure of an all-powerful aristocracy." The colleges of the United States had to "teach what people will pay for learning" and that meant emphasizing "the application of science to the arts" (Wayland, II, 1867, pp. 41, 42, 70, 79–84; Bush, 1891, p. 82).

To apply all the branches of learning to practice would adapt the course of instruction "to the wants of the whole community." Wayland wished to attract to Brown all those who sought such knowledge, particularly the productive classes. Like J. W. Draper in New York, he dreamed of seeing mechanics throng to the university. To that end he offered classes in chemistry to the calico printers and on precious metals to the jewelry-makers of Providence. A similar vision in 1860 induced Yale to offer farmers a short course in agriculture (Wayland, I, 1867, p. 206, II, pp. 89ff., 100ff.; Slosson, 1910, p. 40).

Suddenly necessity, seen in this light, became a virtue. High endowments and good faculty salaries were undesirable because they turned the colleges into "places of literary leisure, and intellectual indolence" and thus retarded rather than advanced the progress of science. While it was "well to revere the genius of Milton, and Dante, and Goethe," Wayland explained, there was "talent in a cotton mill as well as in an epic." He had often been impressed, as he stood in the midst of the clattering machinery, "with the thought, How great an expenditure of mind has been required to produce these spindles, and looms, and engines!" Besides, the advance of civilization was fundamentally due to "inventions in the mechanical arts" (Wayland, II, 1867, p. 105; 1837, pp. 132–135).

But efforts such as Wayland's to frame parallel programs without formal requirements and to encourage part-time study were not notably successful as long as they did not lead to the award of a degree. The search for the means of increasing the number of students therefore led to the incorporation of practical or scientific courses into the regular program. In some universities, enrollment in the professional faculties far outdistanced that in the college, an indication that a vocational value might add weight to the B.A. The growth of technical schools was also impressive. The demands of industry, the railroads, the army and the navy for qualified, skilled personnel had, at first, been met by the creation of separate institutes and academies as in France and Germany; but some universities soon were drawn to expansion in the same direction.[10]

Public pressure hastened them onward. A committee of the Massachusetts Legislature in 1850 concluded that Harvard failed "to answer the just expectations of the people of the State." The committee urged abandonment of the aristocratic literary subjects so that boys who wished to become better farmers, mechanics or merchants could get "specific learning for a specific purpose." The recommendation that salary vary with the number of students a professor attracted had the same purpose, to assure "that those only would succeed who taught in departments, and in a manner acceptable to the public. That which was desired would be purchased, and that which was not, would be neglected" (Morison, 1936b, p. 287).

[10] Porter, 1870, pp. 9ff., 12ff., 14ff.; Wayland, II, 1867, p. 107; Rudolph, 1962, p. 123; Stillé, 1878, p. 131; Richardson & Clark, 1878, pp. 211ff., 364ff.

The response of the colleges varied according to their circumstances. Trinity College for a time offered courses in agriculture and surveying. Oberlin, Notre Dame, and Villanova, among others, experimented with schemes of manual training which had the added advantage of allowing students to work while learning, thus giving "to the mind that strength and independence which always results from the proud consciousness of self-support." Maryland responded to the demand for practical training "adapted to the needs of the mercantile community" by offering courses in engineering, Spanish, and Italian; and Tulane, for the same reason, appointed J. D. B. DeBow professor of commerce. Oberlin, in setting up a "Ladies Course," also promised to "furnish the instruction in the *useful* branches taught in the best female seminaries." Lafayette undertook to train teachers in return for a state grant of $4,000.[11]

The experiments quickly fizzled out. After a few years' trial in each institution, it was generally enough to announce, as a speaker did at Harvard in 1853, that "the students in the college course to-day are all students of science. They are made to remember that history is a science, and that literature, political economy, and ethics are sciences as well as arts." The definition of *scientific,* like that of *practical,* could stretch to fit whatever a faculty wished to offer under that label. Parents wanted it both ways: their sons were to acquire "some degree of Classical Merit" but were also "ever to remember that Knowledge is useless to the possessor and to the world til it is Reduced to practice." And, in the last analysis, students who were prospective lawyers, physicians, merchants, or planters proved no more interested in French, manual training, or natural history than in Greek, divinity, or logic.[12]

The experiments were, after all, unrelated to the functions of the university as most Americans understood them. The college was to train the nation's future leaders. An influential Yale report of 1828 explained that it would shape men "of large and liberal views, of those solid and elegant attainments," which would raise its graduates "to a higher distinction, than the mere possession of property" could give, and would enable them "to move in the more intelligent

[11] Fairchild, 1878, pp. 322, 326, 327; Power, 1958, p. 59; March, 1878, pp. 283–286; Brocklesby, 1878, p. 265; Callcott, 1966, pp. 96, 97; Dyer, 1966, p. 26; Millis, 1927, pp. 16ff., 37, 145ff.

[12] Bush, 1891, pp. 111ff., 259ff.; Pomfret, 1932, p. 145; Wayland, II, 1867, pp. 96, 97; Fairchild, 1878, p. 323; Callcott, 1966, p. 97; Winchester, 1878, p. 313; March, 1878, pp. 286, 287; Schmidt, 1930, p. 89.

circles with dignity, and to make such an application of their wealth, as will be most honorable to themselves, and most beneficial to their country" ("Original Papers," 1829, pp. 323–324).

**IN LOCO PARENTIS**  In the light of such purposes, concern about the curriculum was subsidiary to the task of inculcating moral discipline. "All that remained," Wayland acknowledged after the failure of his reforms at Brown, "was to raise the standard of scholarship in the college, constituted as it then was, and to improve, to the utmost of our power, its discipline and moral character" (Wayland, I, 1867, pp. 207, 222).

That was no mean assignment. The experience of the University of North Carolina in 1851 was not unusual: its student body of 230 that year generated 282 cases of the infraction of rules. The faculty records of a small Presbyterian college in Indiana "read much like the blotter of a police court." Homesick boys, shipped away from their families for reasons that were unclear or confused, were likely to be rebellious. "Indulged, petted, and uncontrolled at home, allowed to trample upon all laws, human and divine, at the preparatory school," they came to college, in the judgment of a professor at Davidson in 1855, undisciplined and uncultivated, "yet with exalted ideas of personal dignity, and a scowling contempt for lawful authority, and wholesome restraint" (Battle, I, 1907, p. 627; Millis, 1927, p. 226ff.; Sims, 1885, pp. 80–82; Godbold, 1944, p. 117).

In each college, a minority of rich youngsters, "on the eve of ruin from wayward natures, bad habits, or hereditary tendencies to evil," squandered "their money in eating and drinking." They were to be "watched, borne with, and if possible saved to the world and to their families." The majority, however, were subject mostly to the petty temptations of youth. There was not much "gross sin," but teachers had to be alert to the habits which might harden into vices—prevarication, pilfering, tippling, playing cards, and cursing. Unchecked, such practices might lead to outlandish debts at the oyster house, to duels and, sometimes, to a general reign of lawlessness which spread contagiously from campus to campus.[13]

Yet the fear of damnation had ceased to be an effective restraint

[13] Wayland, I, 1867, p. 32; Rosenberger, 1927, p. 196; Sims, 1885, pp. 83–104; Clark, 1889, p. 40ff.; Vinton, 1878, pp. 106–107; Hitchcock, 1863, p. 318ff.; Quincy, II, 1840, 369ff.; "Glimpses of Old College Life," 1900, p. 222; "The Great Rebellion," 1907, p. 119ff.; note 19, p. 41.

upon misbehavior; "even the young men professing piety kept their religion to themselves." Nor did appeals to the sense of honor and the love of knowledge bear fruit. Presidents who began with a romantic view of the inherent goodness of man were tempted to revert to a belief in natural depravity when they observed the outcome of efforts to govern by the rule of inward principle rather than of outward fear and restraint. As a result, most colleges had to manage their charges by enforcing detailed codes of behavior. Wayland, for example, required the faculty to have apartments in college and to visit the rooms of students at least twice a day. Daily marks were the basis for term grades that would let parents know how their progeny were getting on. Many a professor compelled to supervise the feeding in the refectory concluded that the atmosphere "was too warlike for the placid pursuit of literature." *"Mein Gott!!"* Francis Lieber is said to have exclaimed. "All dis for two tousand dollars."[14]

Such methods of compulsion had limited utility. President Green of Princeton observed with dismay "the fixed, irreconcilable and deadly hostility" of the boys to the college's "system of diligent study, of guarded moral conduct, and of reasonable attention to religious duty." And President Barnard of Columbia sadly concluded in 1870 that there was "no situation in the world in which an individual" was "more completely removed from all effectual restraint, whether the restraint of direct authority or that of public opinion, than within the walls of an American college." When the chips were down, the parents who wished their sons tamed rarely sustained the sanctions applied to the rule breakers. In the eyes of a father, said President Lindsley of the University of Nashville in 1848, each lad was "a high-minded, honorable, brave, generous, good-hearted young gentleman" who scorned subterfuge, meanness and, above all, lying, being in this particular at least, above suspicion, "and like the Pope, infallible," while the faculty were "a parcel of paltry pedants, pedagogues, bigots, charlatans — without feeling, spirit, kindness, honesty or common sense." Few Americans seriously dissented from such judgments, and there was a widespread tendency to wink at college pranks, no matter how

[14] Hollis, I, 1951–1956, p. 189; Wayland, I, 1867, pp. 32, 205–208, 211, 225; Bush, 1891, pp. 187–190, 227, 259; Callcott, 1966, pp. 149, 150; Curti & Carstensen, I, 1949, pp. 173–176; Fairchild, 1878, pp. 328, 333; March, 1878, p. 284; Raymond, I, 1907, p. 159; Collins, 1914, pp. 107–108, 112–113; Rudolph, 1962, p. 108; Schmidt, 1930, p. 78ff.

outrageous (Wertenbaker, 1946, p. 169; Barnard, 1870, p. 28; Schmidt, 1930, p. 87).

In the running battle to maintain some semblance of orderly behavior, the presidents and professors resisted any trend that might loosen their control. That doughty liberal Thomas Cooper exclaimed, "Republicanism is good: but the 'rights of boys and girls' are the offspring of Democracy gone mad." Lest unsupervised youths have the leisure for subversive plots, Princeton urged all its students to "spend their vacations at home . . . or when this is inconvenient, that they take boarding elsewhere than in Princeton." The university catalog warned that when young persons were "collected together without regular occupation or study, the temptations to idleness and dissipation" were often too strong to be resisted. For the same reason, Wayland, in a tone reminiscent of Increase Mather more than a century earlier, warned the promoters of a new college "not to erect dormitory buildings for students" in which most of the troubles of the faculty had their origin. Benjamin Rush and Manasseh Cutler, distinguished founders of other colleges, also advised against the construction of such "secret nurseries of every vice and the cages of unclean birds." President Hitchcock of Amherst summed up the prevailing faculty opinion in 1863. He knew that parents believed it "safer to the morals of students to have them congregated in large dormitory buildings than to be scattered through the community." But his "own observation for many years" led to the opposite conclusion. Young men were in greatest danger when they were "isolated from public inspection entirely among their own kith and kin, with whom it is a point of honor not to reveal the delinquencies and immoralities of their fellows."[15]

**STUDENT LIFE**  The ability of students to organize autonomously, which their teachers feared, did grow, although not in a form anyone anticipated. Occasional efforts to induce students to discipline themselves through their own courts or legislatures were not notably successful, for these devices were too obviously contrived by the faculty. For the great majority of young men who passed through it, the college was a social experience, shaped not by their elders or by

---

[15] Hollis, I, 1951–1956, p. 89; *Catalogue of the Officers and Students,* 1846, p. 22; Wayland, II, 1867, p. 70; Morgan, 1933, p. 11; Hoover, 1954, p. 16; Cutler, II, 1888, p. 31; Hitchcock, 1863, p. 144; Adams, 1878, p. 347; Cowley, 1934, pp. 710–711.

the subject matter of instruction, but by contact with their peers. That was why all efforts such as those of Ticknor at Harvard, Marsh at Vermont, and Fisk at Wesleyan to classify students by proficiency in courses rather than by length of time in attendance failed. The primary unit was and remained the class, the group that entered together, passed together from status to status—freshman, sophomore, junior, and senior—and celebrated commencement together (Winchester, 1878, p. 308; March, 1878, p. 285; Hitchcock, 1863, pp. 157ff., 318–319).

Everywhere the common experiences of the class were the organizing elements of the life of the students, and these to a considerable degree were free of the oversight of elders. The youths were subject to fits of enthusiasm. The political interests of the revolutionary era sustained some radical fervor down through the end of the eighteenth century. Boys then read Tom Paine, burned the Bible, and toyed with atheism. There followed a turn to religion. The Society of Brethren at Williams was the first of some hundred missionary clubs that had appeared by 1850. When periodic revivals swept through the campus, as at Denison, "seven or eight of as wild boys as were in the college, broke down, and sobbing, begged" their fellows to pray for them. In the decades before the Civil War religious interests also led some enthusiasts into reform movements. [16]

Sooner or later within each college narrower circles of students associated, either to pursue common interests or to achieve a sense of identity by virtue of passage through a selection process. The literary societies, the first of which had been founded at Yale in 1753, served both purposes. Their debates, libraries, and publications were often more effective modes of study than the formal academic exercises; and their ability to exclude some students gave gratifying recognition of the distinction of those admitted. [17]

The longing for fraternity and for an autonomously created pattern of order in time became justification enough for association even without a literary or intellectual content. Students were interested in "lodges" before the end of the eighteenth century, and

---

[16] Chessman, 1957, pp. 81–82; Morison, 1936b, pp. 184, 185; Wertenbaker, 1946, pp. 127, 134–137, 156; Hollis, I, 1951–1956, p. 53; Shedd, 1934, pp. 25ff., 48ff.; Rudolph, 1962, pp. 38, 39, 72, 73; Durfee, 1860, p. 167; Millis, 1927, p. 238ff.

[17] Kingsley, 1878, p. 72; Sims, 1885, p. 106; Millis, 1927, p. 230ff.; Morison, 1936b, pp. 180ff., 202ff., 310ff.

the discipline the faculty could not administer occasionally could be imposed by the young men themselves. The literary societies in some colleges evolved into convivial organizations with codes of behavior internally set. Elsewhere, the old groups lost ground after 1825 to the Greek letter fraternities, which provided living quarters, an election process, and a ritual relatively free of faculty control. The criterion for admitting a new member in 1836 — "Would you want your sister to marry him?" — showed the relationship students desired. They sought a surrogate family, that intimate group life out of which would grow "those delightful associations and those lifelong friendships which add so much to the glory of college days, and which, after all, are the only things to which students love to revert in after years." The spread of these associations in the colleges ran parallel to the spread of Masonic and other secret fraternal orders in American society at large and was due to much the same reasons — the desire for comradeship of isolated individuals in loosely organized and mobile communities.[18]

Few presidents failed to perceive the advantages of the fraternities, which took the college out of the lodging business, freed capital for other uses, and spared the faculty the tasks of supervision. Yet few were also willing to shirk entirely the disciplinary duties expected of them or to run the risk of allowing conspiracies to develop within the student societies. Most compromised. On the one hand, college administrations set up stringent general rules of behavior and absolutely forbade membership in secret societies; on the other hand, they learned to interpret those regulations with a good deal of leniency (*Catalogue of the Officers and Students,* 1846, p. 23).

The dangers of punctiliously insisting upon governing student life nowhere became clearer than at Jefferson's University of Virginia. From the start fear of student violence kept the faculty on edge. But when the boys organized an independent military company and announced that they would resist the "tyrannical movements of the faculty" which ordered them to remove all arms from the campus, the teachers in 1836 out of desperation or boldness ordered a substantial number of expulsions. Two days of rioting ended in compromise: the appearance of the militia upheld the majesty of the law and the retreat of the faculty readmitted the

---

[18] Pomfret, 1932, pp. 138, 142, 143; Fletcher, I, 1943, pp. 444–447; Rudolph, 1956, p. 103; Rosenberger, 1927, pp. 188–189; Handlin, 1961, p. 117ff.; Rudolph, 1962, p. 144ff.; Millis, 1927, pp. 234ff., 240ff.

offending students. Ironically, the professor who engineered the compromise was shot to death by a student four years later.[19]

More than a decade after the event, President Wayland, in the course of a visit to Charlottesville, stood reflectively on the spot where the murder had occurred. He had suffered through his own share of riots and rowdyism at Brown and understood "that the government of impulsive, thoughtless young men" differed from that of adults and had to "of necessity, be kind, conciliatory, persuasive, or, in a word, parental." The college was, he knew, "an intermediate place between the family and society, to prepare the student for entrance upon the practical duties of life." A firm administrator had to juggle his obligations to society, his responsibility for obedience to state law, and his need to satisfy parents, as well as his interests in the students. He could hope for no more than a tolerable equilibrium among those elements (Wayland, I, 1867, pp. 262–264; II, p. 93).

Wayland fully understood the colleges' dilemma. Americans used these institutions for reasons they did not admit to themselves — to control their sons — and fell back upon inflated rhetoric to describe the purpose of the college. As a result, the colleges which "obeyed the suggestions of the public," failed "to find themselves sustained by the public. The means which it was supposed would increase the number of students, in fact diminished it, and thus things gradually, after every variety of trial, have generally tended to their original" character. "And thus have we been taught that the public does not always know what it wants, and that it is not always wise to take it at its word" (Wayland, 1842, p. 13).

Tolerance of the fraternities and other societies as a large area in which students organized their lives without interference from the college took the edge off the conflict between the generations. The growing interest in athletics had the same result. Physical training and gymnastics had been introduced in the 1820s by professors like Carl Follen "to work the devil out of the students." The motto of the Amherst gymnasium (1860) expressed their intention: "Keep thyself pure; the body is the temple of the Holy Ghost." But in the 1850s the emphasis had already begun to shift to team sports and to intercollegiate competition. The growing popularity of baseball in the next decade completed the transition.

---

[19] Patton, 1906, pp. 116ff., 131ff., 143–161. For accounts of other rebellions, see Clark, 1889, pp. 43ff., 51ff.; Morison, 1936b, p. 252ff.; Durfee, 1860, pp. 85, 86; note 13, p. 36.

The mass of students became spectators rather than participants, the games became fiercely competitive, and in the process some youthful aggressiveness was displaced from the faculty at home to the rivals at other colleges.[20]

The ambiguities of purpose and self-justification were the common elements among the American colleges and universities in 1870. These institutions had come into existence for a variety of reasons and in some respects differed markedly—in resources, quality of faculty, religious orientation, regional characteristics, relationship to government, age and social level of their students. The similarities—in the style of life and the running tension between faculty and students—sprang from the unrecognized and scarcely articulated function all colleges were expected to perform. Beneath the grandiloquent talk of republican culture and democratic education lay a simple need of many families. Whatever else institutions of higher education in the United States might aspire to be, their first responsibility was to supply some youths with the training for life in society, training which their parents were unable or unwilling to impart directly. The colleges can hardly be said to have met fully the requirements of that responsibility in 1870, when they were beset by a new range of problems generated by radical change in the society in which they operated.

[20] Brubacher and Rudy, 1958, p. 50; LeDuc, 1946, p. 130; Wayland, I, 1867, p. 224; Rudolph, 1962, p. 151ff.

# 4. The Custodians of Culture, 1870–1930

Between 1870 and 1930, the number of American institutions of higher education increased from somewhat more than 500 to above 1,400. That growth was less significant, however, than the rise in total enrollment from 52,000 to more than 1,100,000. There were more colleges in existence, and they were larger, less fragile, and less poverty-stricken than formerly. Their strength was a product of changes in the whole society and in the particular clientele they expected to serve (Bureau of the Census, 1957, pp. 210–211).

In the period of high industrialization after 1870, the economy of the United States shifted from an agricultural, rural base to an urban, factory-oriented one. The new system of production functioned on a national scale through large, complex organizations and it depended upon the labor of an industrial proletariat, much of it foreign-born. Quickly, the society that Jefferson, Jackson, and even Lincoln had known became but a memory. A totally new setting for life was the context for the development of American higher education.

From its clerical antecedents, the college before 1870 had inherited the function of inculcating traditional morality in the age group not yet subject to the controls of society and yet already beyond the reach of parental discipline. The college had thus protected the outside world against disruption by reckless young people, whom it thereby absolved from the necessity of assuming full responsibility for their actions. Its religious, scholarly, and vocational aims had all been intertwined with this quasi-parental role. The altered context of life in the United States after 1870 compelled the college to make far-reaching adjustments in the performance of that role in order to accommodate altered views of the moral code it sustained and the novel situation of the students it sheltered. Yet the validity of the conception of the college as an instrument of socialization survived and, indeed, gained strength.

**THE SOCIAL CONTEXT OF HIGHER EDUCATION** After 1870, traditional morality no longer provided an adequate sanction either for social experience in general or for the discipline of the colleges. In the decade after the publication of *Origin of Species,* Darwinism made subtle inroads upon American thought. Its impact was greatest among the best educated, and the colleges therefore were particularly susceptible to its influence. The erosion of the familiar Christian view of the creation and the destiny of the universe cut the ground out from beneath the belief in the uniqueness of man's role as the central actor in a divine drama. He was but a creature shaped by the environment, one who struggled, like others, for survival and for a quite unknowable purpose.

Significant social influences added to the intellectual pressure toward change in attitudes toward morality. The codes of behavior derived from traditional wisdom, which for centuries had proved adaptable to a variety of conditions, did not accommodate themselves so readily to a milieu, the most prominent features of which were large organizations, heavy industry, and metropolitan cities. The faith in the old fundamentals remained vital in the rural regions least subject to change. But in the dynamic, urban sectors of American life, even occasional outbursts of evangelical fervor could not bring the old-time religion to life or turn it into a reliable guide to personal or social conduct (Veblen, 1965, pp. 8–9).

Science was the potent rival of religion. The knowledge derived from scholarship gained steadily in prestige, and the claims for its validity quickly spread from the physical and natural realms to the social and personal ones, which had formerly been the exclusive domain of religion. The development of sociology, economics, law, politics, and psychology as sciences created new standards for behavior which sometimes clashed with the ethical norms derived from religious sources. Popular willingness to accept any novelty to which the designation *science* was attached gave this rivalry far-reaching implications.

The position of the colleges was ambiguous. As institutions, they were heirs of the old kind of truth; yet their staffs increasingly expounded the new. President James McCosh, traveling to take up his post at Princeton in 1868, felt the weight of the dilemma which resulted from that ambiguity as he pondered whether or not to avow his receptivity to Darwinism. He did speak out, at the cost of having his orthodoxy impugned, and thus began the process of "inevitable compromise" between the old and the new beliefs (White, I, 1896, p. 80; Collins, 1914, pp. 222–223).

The phrase "inevitable compromise" came from the retrospective account of Andrew D. White, another college president who confronted similar issues. The adjustment was a compromise in the sense that it plastered together professions of loyalty to the old morality and the objective knowledge of the new science. The day was far from over when a professor could be instructed to teach biology "as an absolutely dependent product of an absolutely independent and spiritual Creator." Yet the adjustment was inevitable because the scientists in the college had to reconcile pursuit of learning, which might undermine traditional wisdom, with their role as mentors of youth preparing for places in a society frankly unwilling to cut loose from familiar views. And the promoters of universities, for whom the essential was "to get the structure up," did not trouble themselves overly about questions of abstract purpose as long as they "made the dirt of learning fly" (LeDuc, 1946, pp. 83–86; Benn, 1928, pp. 38–39).

Uncertainty about its own role deepened the college's vulnerability to external pressures. Its clientele—primarily the parents of its students—made two insistent demands upon higher education, neither entirely new, yet each endowed with a fresh urgency after 1870. The college was charged with preparing its graduates for careers and also with transmitting to them a code of behavior not grounded upon religious doctrine, yet in some vague and undefined manner preserving Christian values.

Industrialization altered the structure of opportunities available to young people. Whether the chances of a rise in status were greater or lesser than formerly was not as important as the appearance of new kinds of tensions associated with mobility which, in the United States, directly affected attitudes toward education. The stories of the new men of great wealth were familiar enough to Americans of the gilded age. So too, though less frequently discussed, were the stories of the new poor—the bankrupt merchant, the foreclosed farmer, the clerk rendered jobless by recurrent depression, the tramps who crowded the country roads or urban lodging houses. The rewards of success were fabulous and the penalties of failure totally disastrous. The widening gap between the two possible outcomes increased the hazards of competition in a dynamic and therefore unstable society.

Anxious parents, considering the future of their sons and able to do something to guard against the plunge downward if not to assure the climb upward, gradually realized that the most vital sectors of the economy were no longer controlled by inheritance, with secure places passed along within the family. Nor were desirable occupations open, as in the old frontier days, to any would-be entrant. The activities which had once been organized about the household or the family shrank in importance. Land ownership and the pursuit of agriculture ceased to be significant channels for upward movement or even means for retaining a desirable status in society. At best, in certain stable situations, land gave established families a means of standing still while the world marched by. In trade and industry, the impersonal corporation steadily replaced the family firm. A few crafts to which apprenticeship had been the accepted mode of entry retained their vitality and their control over the admission of new members through powerful unions—in construction, printing, and railroading, for instance. But those occupations also were static and most other crafts sank into rapid decay.

By contrast, the most desirable places were those increasingly defined as professions, to which the access was by a process of growing formality involving education. The expectation gradually spread that entry to the practice of law, medicine, and engineering and into large areas of corporate enterprise would come not by inheritance or apprenticeship, but rather by passage through a defined course of formal training in an institution of higher learning. A combination of needs fed that expectation: the desire for credentials in a complex society of large organizations, the difficulty of recruiting and identifying talent for very specialized tasks, and the reluctance of the consumers of technical services to rely upon purely pragmatic judgments of competence. But in addition the development of a formal succession of steps into these desirable callings gave some sense of security to parents able to put their sons through it.

The appearance of professional and, particularly, of graduate schools of law, medicine, business, and engineering was both evidence of the process of formalization and also a stimulus that confirmed it. The antecedents of these faculties reached back to the early nineteenth century, but they had then been only loosely connected to the university and they had not been the usual mode of entry to any calling. Both circumstances changed after 1870; professional schools were integral parts of universities and became the common means of acquiring certain vocations. Increasingly the important element in the life of ambitious young men was admission to such a course of training.

The rapid multiplication of universities and of professional faculties within them tended, however, to diminish the value of the credentials they awarded. Despite the restrictive efforts of various professional societies, the M.D. and LL.B. were as easy to come by, and as uncertain in value, as admission to practice had been earlier. The institutions able to raise their standards and thereby to enhance the value of their degrees among discriminating consumers did so, on the one hand, by improving the quality of instruction and, on the other, by stiffening admission requirements, often hinging them on the previous completion of a collegiate program. By the end of the century ambitious young men understood that, while there were many ways of becoming a physician or lawyer, places on the staffs of the best hospitals and firms went to graduates of a few professional schools, which in turn demanded a good bachelor's degree for admission. "You should connect yourself with a well-known and prosperous institution," was the advice to youth, "for much the same reason that you should seek connection with a strong business house or professional firm." Otherwise, "you will find yourself carrying the college instead of the college carrying you." A Harvard degree in 1871 had cash value even in Chicago.[1]

The fact that professional schools in the United States, unlike those in Europe, were postgraduate imposed a selective function on the undergraduate college and increased the enrollments of the most prestigious institutions. Harvard, Yale, and some of their rivals, thus enabled to choose among applicants, in turn imposed the pressure of their admission requirements upon the "abjectly servile" secondary schools, so that subtle influence from above

[1] Canfield, 1902, pp. 8–9, 25–26, 157; Adams, 1918, p. 305; Veblen, 1965, p. 5; Bishop, 1962, p. 384; Hadley, 1895, pp. 67, 72; Norton, 1895, p. 11; Matthews, 1895, p. 166.

exerted a homogenizing effect upon curricula throughout the nation.[2]

As a result, a tightly articulated formal educational system replaced the loosely patterned arrangements of earlier times. The process was not altogether complete in 1930; but by that date the normal expectation was fixed that students would regularly pass upward through four tiers, each smaller than that below it and each therefore selective and competitive—elementary, secondary, collegiate and professional. The role of the college within this structure was critical to an influential sector of society, for it controlled access to places of increasing importance in the whole economy.

Prolongation of the educational process steadily raised the age of the college students, to the growing concern of administrators. Expedients like the quarter term, the summer session and the combined arts-professional program were not effective in halting the trend. A perceptive observer, describing the hostility of parents and students to such innovations, explained: "Not only do they want the degree, but they want it on the date when it is supposed to fall due."[3]

The insistence upon a regular date of entry and exit revealed that the importance of the college sprang not only from its place in the unfolding career of the individual, but also from its role in the development of the age group in which he found himself. Increasingly Americans tended to divide the life of the person not yet an adult into fixed time spans, correlated with the stages of education. Infancy was a period of pure play and of such preparation as a kindergarten might give for what would follow. Childhood between the ages of 6 and 14 was the beginning of formal learning at the elementary level; and adolescence, from 14 to 18, was properly spent in the high school. The growing hostility to child labor reflected an assumption that all girls and boys passed through the identical stages and ought therefore to enjoy the same schooling.

There was no such certainty about the interval between the ages of 18 and 22. People of that age were not children, not even adolescents. But, in the middle and upper social groups, neither were

[2] Hall, 1923, p. 352; Morison, 1936b, p. 368ff.; Sloane, 1895, p. 118; Henderson, 1912; Broome, 1903; Fuess, 1950; Benn, 1928, pp. 29–36; Handlin, 1959.

[3] Churchman, 1912, p. 27; Matthews, 1895, pp. 179–183; Norton, 1895, pp. 11, 17; Canfield, 1902, p. 36ff.

they adults, expected to enter life fully as heads of families and citizens. A society oriented toward the hope of upward social mobility offered inducements for the postponement of the age of marriage with its attendant obligations until careers were fixed and the capital accumulated for an establishment at an appropriate station. This was hardly a problem for the great majority of resourceless workers or farmers. But families with some margin faced a significant choice when a son approached the age of 18 and left high school. They supplied the college with students.

Increasingly such families came to consider the four years after the age of 18 a period not for occupational training, but for further preparation before arriving at a decision about future vocation, that is, a period for college. "That's what education does," explains the father in a story, "—knocks all the vagueness out of a young chap." Clearly this "mountain ridge" to be crossed to adulthood— an interval without precise purpose—was more equably passed away from, than at, home. By 1907, a president's report noted, "Rich parents send their sons to college as in summers they send them to the seashore or to the mountains," that is, as a stage of separation. The wealthy were not alone in doing so. "Parents, whose hard-working lives have always spelled duty, choose each year to beat their way against rigid economy, penury, and bitter loss, that their sons may possess what they themselves never had, a college education." Such offspring, George Santayana observed, were "fond, often compassionately fond, of their parents" and home was "all the more sacred to them in that they" were seldom there.[4]

The college student was expected to gain not so much technical or professional competence as "general culture," a vague concept identified with the command of a pattern of manners and a body of knowledge—generally classical in antecedents—which, since the eighteenth century at least, had been the marks of distinction of the gentlemanly elite.[5]

The role of the college as custodian of culture gained strength, after 1870, from English influences associated with Matthew Arnold, from some strands of German university life, and from the incorporation of science, with all its pragmatic prestige, into the

[4] Montross, 1923, p. 61; Bishop, 1962, p. 403; Cooper, 1912, pp. 8, 192, 195; Santayana, 1934, p. 45; Hall, 1901, p. 97.

[5] Sloane, 1895, p. 129; Cooper, 1912, p. 66; Canfield, 1902, p. 40ff.; Fisher, 1917, p. 16ff.

roster of subjects taught. The function of the college was "to draw out, stimulate, and strengthen the intellectual powers, to cultivate taste and sensibility for the finest art and literature" and to impart "a thoroughly scientific acquaintance" with all the branches of learning. By "breathing the atmosphere of culture" the student became a "whole man" and fitted himself "for the battle of life" (Collins, 1914, pp. 226–227; Matthews, 1895, p. 182; Perry, 1922, p. 213).

**CUSTODIANS OF CULTURE**  Culture replaced religion as the guide to thought, behavior and emotion. The American universities did not become antireligious or unchristian; and there was still much concern for the teaching of ethics, the "topwork of man's structure." But, except for the surviving sectarian institutions, the college, though "required by public opinion to have religion—in a general way, somehow," was nevertheless "forbidden to have it in any particular way." Repeatedly educators called for the development of the type of man that the world most needed, "the cultured citizen in command of scientific methods." By producing such a man the college could "incorporate the spirit of the times in the spirit of the fathers."[6]

Without the guidelines the college undertook to supply, society unmoored from traditional faith was at the mercy of quacks and imposters. "The astrologer in the Middle Ages was a rare personage," wrote President Charles W. Eliot of Harvard, "but now he advertises in the public newspapers and flourishes as never before. Men and women of all classes . . . seek advice . . . from clairvoyants, seers, Christian Scientists, mind-cure practitioners . . . and fortune tellers. The ship of state barely escapes from one cyclone of popular folly, like the fiat-money delusion or the granger legislation of the seventies, when another blast of ill-informed opinion comes down on it, like the actual legislation which compels the buying and storing of silver by Government." The university would validate the proper theories in all fields of knowledge and certify to its graduates the correct views on the issues of life they would later face. It would thus produce a corps of educated leaders prepared to give guidance to the whole society.[7]

This function was particularly important in the United States

[6] Goodstein, 1962, p. 225; Fleming, 1936, p. 225; Slosson, 1910, p. 57; Santayana, 1934, p. 58ff.

[7] Eliot, 1892, pp. 411, 412, 417, 423, 427; Eliot, 1903, p. 46ff.; Bishop, 1962, p. 153; Cooper, 1912, p. 59ff.

where a characteristic separation had developed "between things intellectual, which remain wrapped in a feminine veil and, as it were, under glass, and the rough business and passions of life." The university had to exert a "counter influence against the excessive commercial spirit, and against the chicanery and selfishness of demagoguism." It had to resist the prevailing tendency toward materialism and "mercantile morality," because it was the "one community which for a considerable period" took "into its keeping many of the most susceptible and most promising" of the nation's "youth, to impart to them better tastes, higher aims, and, above all, to teach them to despise all sorts of intellectual and moral shams." Insofar as it was a custodian of culture, its task was, as Matthew Arnold explained, to produce "sweetness and light," not miners or engineers or architects. Whatever other motives may also have swayed them, it was primarily to acquire culture in that non-vocational sense that students and their parents turned to the college.[8]

In the United States, which lacked a hereditary aristocracy and legally defined symbols of status, families of wealth and power sought to achieve social recognition of their superiority through the possession of culture. The college, especially the proper college, was one of a cluster of institutions which validated their claims. "Many parents who have acquired riches rapidly, and are desirous of obtaining social position and consideration for their sons, send them to college for this end," Charles Eliot Norton observed. Or, as a less friendly critic put it, the college bestowed upon the well-to-do "a sort of petty tyranny" within which they could "dominate the social activities of the people" as the aristocracy of Europe did.

Such fears, while grounded in reality, were exaggerated. The would-be aristocrats were mostly to be disappointed; the society was too fluid to permit them to maintain control or permanently to dominate the culture. Every "mom" in a western hick town who sent her son off to college "had visions of him returning from Chicago or New York in an English ulster and a velour hat, carrying a sleek bag—very dignified, a bit pompous and yet extremely gracious, sweeping her into his arms with the exclamation, 'Little Mother!' then sitting down to outline to her the colossal schemes of his big business in the East." The increase in the number of col-

[8] Santayana, 1934, p. 44; Tappan, 1951, p. 66; Porter, 1870, p. 182; Bishop, 1962, pp. 40ff., 177, 178; Norton, 1895, p. 36; Cooper, 1912, pp. 58, 99; Angell, 1928, p. 4.

leges and their success in imitating one another offset the exclusionary and discriminatory practices that developed in the most sought-after schools. The pursuit of culture could not be contained within a narrow group; the hope of attaining the distinction conveyed by the bachelor's degree attracted a growing host of young men and women of moderate means.[9]

The concept of the college as a custodian of culture encountered early and prolonged, although in the end unsuccessful, opposition. Many Americans who insisted that all forms of expression be native, real, manly, and down-to-earth reacted with instinctive aversion to the East, which they considered but an extension of Europe, and to gentility, which they considered but another name for effete, dudish snobbery. Suspicion of the foreign, aristocratic influences gained force from the Populist strain, not unmixed with envy, that entered the thinking of professors such as V. L. Parrington, J. Allen Smith, or Thorstein Veblen, as well as from the writers, Mark Twain to Theodore Dreiser, who challenged conventional academic standards.

More generally, hostility to the college's dedication to its own definition of culture ran counter to the century-old conviction that education had to be immediately useful and practical. Appeals for aid from the public purse rested upon the justification of utility; that was the spirit of the Morrill Act and of the foundation of new institutes of technology and state universities. The same justification was also in accord with widespread democratic assumptions. To President James B. Angell of Michigan nothing could be "more hateful, more repugnant to our natural instincts, more calamitous at once to learning and to the people, more unrepublican, more undemocratic, more unchristian" than restriction of "the priceless boon of higher education to the rich." It was because he wished to open opportunities to poor young men that Ezra Cornell founded what he hoped would be "an institution where any person can find instruction in any study"; for the same reason he wished it to function as a kind of trade school through which deserving youths could work their way (Angell, 1879, p. 11; Bishop, 1962, pp. 56ff., 62ff., 73–74, 87ff., 121, 126–128, 308).

But even Ezra Cornell was not quite clear about what kind of institution it would be that could do what he wished it to. On the

[9] Norton, 1895, p. 16; Crane, 1909, pp. 37ff., 114; Montross, 1923, p. 27; Handlin, O. & M., 1956, pp. 1–7; Veblen, 1965, pp. 74, 87–89; Angell, 1928, p. 19ff.

one hand, he drew up plans for college-operated shoe and chair factories and actually instituted a printing plant to keep the students busy; on the other hand, he wanted "a university of the first magnitude — such as we have to go to Europe to find." Andrew D. White, the president, was less unclear. He had no intention of flouting his principal benefactor, but located the emphasis somewhat differently: the new university would train not the rank and file, but the "captains in the army of industry" with manners polished for their future status. And shortly after Cornell died in 1874, much of the aspiration toward self-help, work, and practicality faded away. Before long Ithaca was being described as another haven of the children of the rich. At other institutions also it was quite consistent to maintain that "a college organized without reference to the needs of society has no meaning" and to argue from that premise that its function was to develop the capacity of men of "superior talent" to be leaders in the service of society (Bishop, 1962, pp. 128, 178, 202, 247, 352, 441; Dartmouth College, 1924, part I, pp. 10, 15).

·A similar trend operated in the state universities. Deans and presidents, of course, assured grumbling legislators that their purpose was "to make the farms prosperous and happy and enable them to compete with the cities for the best talent of the land." But the conception of training "fancy farmers" or "fancy mechanics" had little attractiveness for the men in the factories or in the fields who believed that an introduction "to a pair of heavy neat's leather boots and corduroy pants" and a lesson in loading manure was a better way of teaching agriculture than a class in the laboratory. The way to keep boys down on the farm was not to send them away.[10]

The state universities, like the older colleges, recruited their students from families which were *not* sure that they wanted their offspring to remain on the farm. However strong the rural agrarian ideal remained, higher education in practice was an avenue upward into the professions or business; and increasingly Ann Arbor and Iowa City promised to deliver the same skills and polish — the same evidences of culture — that Cambridge or Princeton did. The faculties, too, at both types of institutions taught much the same subjects in much the same ways. In time, the state universities learned to acquit themselves of their debt to the taxpaying farmers, not so much by course instruction for youth as by the services of

[10] Viles, 1939, p. 298; Eddy, 1957, p. 31; Ross, 1942, p. 91; Crane, 1909, pp. 156–163, 187, 271.

associated agricultural stations made possible by the Hatch Act of 1887, by the spread of extension work, and by the supply of a pool of experts and a body of expertise useful to progressives in government. But the agglomeration of all these functions in a single institution never quite obscured the central educational service it performed, which came more and more to approximate that of the old liberal arts college or university.[11]

The university's function as custodian of culture also affected its receptivity to science. The conviction that knowledge was attainable by the use of reason, applied objectively to evidence gained through research or experiment, exerted novel pressures on scholarship. The day of the learned amateur was all but over; mastery of a subject now called for highly technical skills, for access to extensive libraries and laboratories, and for close communication with peers throughout the world. Science became institutionalized, in the sense that it developed an organization by disciplines, internal standards for the accreditation of practitioners and for the validation of results, and a claim for recognition of its competence by society at large.

The influence of Germany made science an activity of the university rather than of autonomous academies, museums, technical schools, institutes, or state agencies, as had been the earlier American expectation. But to provide a setting congenial for scholarship an altogether new kind of university seemed necessary to men like Daniel C. Gilman. First at Berkeley and then at Johns Hopkins he sought to create "a foundation for the promotion and diffusion of knowledge—a group of agencies organized to advance the arts and sciences of every sort, and train young men as scholars for all the intellectual callings of life." President William Rainey Harper at Chicago also believed that the university owed the world a duty, that of research and investigation into all the problems of the age. It could fulfill that duty by providing a center of thought, where the process of exposing error and revealing truth could go on, a law unto itself, "indifferent alike to plaudits or reproaches" and divorced from considerations of immediate utility.[12]

The learned men engaged in that process of scientific inquiry

[11] Notestein, 1937, p. 290; Ross, 1942, pp. 136–151; McCarthy, 1912; True, 1928; Hofstadter & Hardy, 1952, p. 42ff.

[12] Gilman, 1872, p. 6; Gilman, 1885, p. 16; Ryan, 1939, pp. 122, 123; Veblen, 1965, p. 23; Hall, 1923, p. 540; Bishop, 1962, pp. 40, 233ff.; Bush, 1891, pp. 280–287, 320ff.; Sloane, 1895, p. 117.

would hardly find attractive the problems of disciplining unruly and uninterested youth, often the preponderant task of the old-time college in the United States. President Harper charged that the American college system had "actually murdered hundreds of men who while in its service" felt "that something more must be done than the work of the classroom" and who therefore either shriveled intellectually or "died from overwork." It seemed crucial to him, as to the other founders of the new institutions, decisively to remove the scientific researchers from undergraduate instruction. The divorce could be achieved either through separate faculties or through an associated school that would feed candidates into the process of graduate study or through the refusal to admit any students except those prepared for advanced work. In any case it was essential to maintain a clear distinction between *collegiate* and *university* work. The old colleges would have to turn into universities of the new sort, or sink to the level of secondary schools, or lose all reason for existence. [13]

However logical that clear-cut resolution seemed in anticipation, it did not come to pass. Instead, undergraduate instruction almost everywhere remained intertwined with the scholarly activities of the university. This outcome was partly the result of the situation of the state universities, which grew not selectively but through the agglomeration of functions and therefore simply thrust graduate teaching upon the same faculty already responsible for undergraduates. But the association of the two kinds of learning also had a justification in the concept of the university-college advocated by Charles W. Eliot, among others. The institution that was to be the custodian of culture had to bring together the future leaders of society and "the best attainable instruction in those studies by which knowledge may be increased, the level of intellectual life elevated, and the consequent moral improvement of the community secured." Graduate research, ever refining and redefining the correct answers to the problems of art, literature, the social order, and the material world, capped the whole educational system, to which its link was the college (Norton, 1895, pp. 23, 30–32; Ryan, 1939, pp. 132–133).

The association between the general culture communicated in

[13] Harper, 1905, p. 107; Burgess, 1884, p. 5; Ryan, 1939, pp. 19, 101, 112, 115–116, 140; Bishop, 1962, p. 42; Matthews, 1895, p. 160ff.; Veblen, 1965, p. 17; Jastrow, 1912, p. 495.

the college and the scholarship pursued in the university was so compelling—attractive to faculties and persuasive to alumni and donors—that Johns Hopkins, Clark, Columbia, Stanford, and Chicago, which began with the opposite intentions, found themselves pulled in the same direction. Each made its own compromise with the problem of elementary instruction. On the other hand, parents who believed that "undergraduate work, at least for the first two years," could "be done better in a college than in a great university" continued to send their sons to Amherst, Dartmouth, Oberlin, or Wabash; but even the institutions which prided themselves on their liberal arts character were transformed by the influence of the universities from which they increasingly drew their teaching staffs (Storr, 1966, pp. 127–128, 324; Slosson, 1910, p. 2; Hadley, 1895, pp. 55, 63).

**THE COLLEGE MAN**  There remained exceedingly important differences among American institutions of higher education. Regional variations were striking, as were the distinctive characteristics of the old schools with colonial origins, of the great state universities, of the small sectarian colleges, of institutions with numerous commuting students, and of those with a specialized clientele of Negroes, Catholics, or women. Yet there were also significant similarities among all these types. Despite the tremendous diversity in origin, control, and ostensible purpose, the common elements were even more consequential.

This great variety of institutions, whatever else they did, aimed to produce a single product—the college man. The years spent in college were to endow the graduates with the cultural equipment to distinguish them in the future, not so much through formal courses of instruction as through participation in the way of life of a community.

The model college was therefore residential; the experience was incomplete if it did not take the student away from home. The founders of the new universities, like their predecessors, shied away from the responsibilities of managing dormitories; but like their predecessors, they had to take on the burden, for the supply of housing was otherwise inadequate (Bishop, 1962, pp. 78, 81ff.; Canfield, 1902, p. 67ff.).

The fraternities helped to fill the gap. But the accommodations they provided were not the only reasons for the rapid growth of

these organizations. Although nominally under collegiate supervision, they nevertheless offered their residents a large measure
of self-government and they recognized the actualities of the differences in background, interests and tastes among the students.
Like the secret societies in some places, or the Harvard and Yale
clubs with their links to Boston and New York society, the fraternities everywhere were selective and exclusive as the college as
a whole was not; and they provided a means for organizing within
the university meaningful autonomous subgroupings "composed
of young men drawn from the same station in life, the similarity
of whose past associations and experiences" rendered them mu-
tually agreeable.[14]

In the pleasant interlude of independence that the college bestowed on young men before they were expected to settle down
into the routine of affairs, they were "sympathetically encouraged
to instruct themselves and to educate one another" after their own
fashions. They romped and made fun, had their private brain-
storms like "little supermen" in a haphazard existence without
much form other than that which was self-created. Some men were
active in literary and debating societies; others staffed the newspapers and periodicals. The humorous magazines were particularly
important, not for the talent they evoked, but for the commentary
and mirror they presented to the life about them. A few earnest
or ambitious youths took part in politics, in reform, in socialist
clubs, or in the settlement houses. But by and large, the focus of
activity was the campus rather than the world about it.[15]

While it offered enough latitude to allow almost every type of
student to go his own way, the college was also consciously a whole
community — "one family, socially considered," as Harper put it —
and it made an effort to express its wholeness physically, intellectually, and ceremoniously. The plant, from this point of view,
acquired a novel significance. Endowments and income were now
sufficiently large so that many institutions were no longer guided
in building solely by considerations of economy and function.
Architecture acquired an aesthetic and social purpose; the halls

[14] Flandrau, 1897, p. 261ff.; Benn, 1928, p. 50ff.; Morison, 1936b, 419ff.; Storr,
1966, p. 170; McCosh, 1878, p. 440.

[15] Santayana, 1934, p. 45; Benn, 1928, pp. 74, 134ff.; Cooper, 1912, p. 59;
Canfield, 1902, p. 118ff.; Angell, 1928, pp. 3, 6, 224; Hall, 1923, p. 83; Feuer,
1969, p. 346; Flandrau, 1897, p. 267ff.

and quadrangles—preferably Gothic or Georgian—were to stand away from the structures in which the world did its work and, like churches, leave an impression of a society apart, with values and loyalties of its own, transmitting a sense of consecration by the "mysterious guidance" of the associations of place.[16]

Other features of college life also fixed upon the student the awareness that he was a member of a distinctive community, "like passengers in a ship or fellow-countrymen abroad" whose "sense of common interests and common emotions overwhelms all latent antipathies." Despite efforts to base progress toward the degree on achievement, the class of entry remained the individual's basic identifying unit. Everywhere there was an attempt to keep the freshmen together in order to establish a common spirit, however much they might divide later. The social events that studded the year had the same purpose and, to the extent that parents and alumni were involved, also strengthened the impression of institutional permanence. A code of conduct was imposed by one undergraduate generation upon another through hazing and initiation rituals, and it was often used by the faculty to govern examinations and classwork. The code rested on the boy's "honor as a gentleman" and thus had vaguely chivalric antecedents; yet it was not snobbish insofar as it respected the student who worked his way through, even at menial tasks like waiting on table. The scions of good family were cautioned that "the student who has been brought up always to dine in a dinner-coat will have for his table-companions men who have never owned a dress coat and who see no immediate prospect of needing one." If college life produced a "tendency to uniformity" in fashions of clothing, tastes and behavior, as Santayana perceived, it also established a kind of order that the otherwise unruly youths imposed on themselves.[17]

After 1870, athletics became the focal point of college life for many students. Certainly this was the impression the lads who read about Stover or Merriwell brought to Yale, or even to *Good Old Siwash.* Intercollegiate football grew steadily in prominence

[16] Storr, 1966, p. 166; Collins, 1914, pp. 252, 279ff.; Benn, 1928, pp. 127, 130; Bishop, 1962, p. 81; Norton, 1895, p. 38.

[17] Pierson, I, 1952, p. 7; Matthews, 1895, p. 181ff.; Crane, 1909, p. 124; Collins, 1914, p. 259; Baldwin, 1915; Benn, 1928, pp. 20–21, 47–49; Cooper, 1912, p. 100; Santayana, 1934, p. 46; McCosh, 1878, p. 439; Angell, 1928, pp. 28ff., 173ff.; Cutting, 1871, p. 133; Bagg, 1871, p. 535.

despite the distasteful professionalism already evident in the 1890s and despite a temporary loss of esteem after the heavy toll of injuries in 1905 (Crane, 1909, p. 129; Rudolph, 1962, p. 373ff.; Morison, 1936b, p. 405ff.).

The initial impetus to athletic programs had come from the desire to provide a harmless means of expending youthful energies; and some presidents continued to believe in a "thorough fatiguing" of the body as a way of keeping students out of trouble. In addition the competitiveness of team sports developed qualities important to advocates of the strenuous life; President Theodore Roosevelt explained the worth of rough play in preventing the colleges from turning out "mollycoddles instead of vigorous men." Football tempered character and diminished drinking; it demonstrated the usefulness of both cooperation and individualism. Indeed, its numerous virtues seemed to the president of Williams in 1908 well on the way to obliterating the difference between a college and "an institute of physical culture."[18]

Beyond this puffing up of the value of competitive sport lay the recognition that the athletic contest was a great ritual event which drew together students and alumni and, in the zest of the effort to beat the other side, developed a consciousness of their identity. The athletes were selfless sufferers straining to do or die for the sake of all; and their sacrifices took "hold of the emotions of the student body in such a way as to make class distinctions relatively unimportant." At Yale it even dissolved the prejudice against the scientific department. On "the foot-ball field, no narrow traditions of college life or college association could prevent the recognition of prowess, the formation of friendships, and the mutual influence on character" of men from different departments.[19]

The athletic contest was the occasion for a display of loyalty akin to patriotism. The massed crowds in the stadium, the show of distinctive colors, the songs, all were evidences of an attachment to the college which it was not ludicrous to juxtapose with that to God and country. It was significant that the youths, here away from home, thought of themselves as sons of an alma mater.

The importance of college life, that is, of immersion in the activ-

---

[18] Geiger, 1958, pp. 238–239; Collins, 1914, p. 226; Bealle, 1948, p. 9; Ryan, 1929, p. 130; Canfield, 1902, p. 110ff.

[19] Benn, 1928, pp. 60–63; Hadley, 1906, p. 452; Hadley, 1895, pp. 64, 89–90; Angell, 1928, p. 5; Hofstadter & Hardy, 1952, p. 112.

ities of a self-contained community, was clearly described in Harold Lloyd's *College Days,* in the popular fiction of the period—of which Owen Wister's *Philosophy 4* was representative—and also in the reminiscences and biographies of the graduates of these years. The bookish types who devoted themselves exclusively to their studies missed the chief value ascribed to the experience.[20]

Discipline under these circumstances presented a difficult problem. The quasi-parental oversight of an earlier period was neither to the taste of faculties composed of men with scholarly interests nor in accord with the wishes of the undergraduates. In establishing Cornell, President White hoped that the professors would not be policemen, but friends of the students, who could govern themselves by a kind of autonomous military organization. Harvard boasted that it subjected its men to the severe test of making them "at once masters of their own lives." Some failed; but the "effect in developing moral character, through the sense of personal responsibility" was, the University believed, "unquestionably beneficial to a great majority." Parents who wished their sons "constrained to virtue by external observances and formal penalties" were told not to send them to Cambridge.[21]

In practice, not even Harvard and Cornell were as permissive as their statements made out; and most institutions insisted that students needed "some sort of oversight when they are away from home." Instructors were not hired "simply to teach Latin or Greek, mathematics or metaphysics." They had a responsibility "in regard to the formation of character and the kindling of spiritual aspirations" as well as of "the conduct of the young men under them." Presidents certainly kept that dual role in mind in making appointments. Furthermore, the college did not exist in a world of its own. Fathers continued to believe that the discipline they themselves could not apply ought—though benevolently—to be administered by the faculty. Above all, since students were not "a privileged class, beyond civil prosecutions," punishment by the college generally fended off more severe action by the criminal authorities (McCosh, 1878, pp. 433, 436–438; Cooper, 1912, p. 74; LeDuc, 1946, p. 26).

[20] Wister, 1903; Hall, 1901, p. 88; Bagg, 1871, p. 701; Freidel, I, 1952, p. 55ff.; Benn, 1928, p. 20; Angell, 1928, p. 2; Bishop, 1962, p. 305ff.

[21] Bishop, 1962, pp. 77, 88, 125; Norton, 1895, pp. 18, 21–22; Cooper, 1912, pp. 147ff., 151; Veblen, 1965, p. 15; Bagg, 1871, p. 588.

The conventional wisdom of the college taught that the essential element in preventing mischief was, "undoubtedly, a well-organized system of instruction, whereby the students are kept busy from day to day." There was no conventional wisdom, alas, to define a well-organized curriculum. Year by year the size of the catalog grew—at Princeton it trebled in the decade of the 1870s, and that institution was not as subject to Teutonic influences as others. The result was utter confusion so long as no ordering principle governed the relationship of various offerings to one another. Yet these same years saw the failure of efforts to develop parallel, different but equal, and coordinate programs and a decline in the number of special students willing to go their own way without candidacy for a degree.[22]

The hopes held out for the lecture system, that it would transform the teacher from a drillmaster into a creative scholar and that it would counteract the danger of too narrow specialization, depended for realization upon sufficient latitude to permit the professor to present a subject he knew thoroughly and yet relieve him "of the presence of a body of students who are compelled to an unwelcome task." Wayland at Brown and White at Cornell had attempted to broaden the range of selection before C. W. Eliot at Harvard popularized the solution as the elective system (Storr, 1966, p. 176; Bishop, 1962, p. 74ff.; *Addresses, Inauguration of Eliot,* 1869, p. 42).

Clearly the new system made scholarship possible among college teachers. But its proponents also had to argue that it was beneficial to students. White early stated the theme: "The attempt to give mental discipline by studies which the mind does not desire is as unwise as to attempt to give physical nourishment by food which the body does not desire." A college man, Eliot explained, "ought to know what he likes best and is most fit for" and therefore could find his own "way to happy, enthusiastic work," through the free play of "natural preferences and inborn aptitudes." The elective process, another president explained, enabled students to select such subjects as would interest them and thus itself forced their minds to act with greatest vigor.[23]

[22] McCosh, 1878, p. 435; Collins, 1914, pp. 228, 255–256; Sloane, 1895, p. 117; Santayana, 1934, p. 55; Slosson, 1910, pp. 40–41; Cooper, 1912, p. 52.

[23] Eliot, 1908, p. 150; Bishop, 1962, p. 74; *Addresses, Inauguration of Eliot,* 1869, p. 39ff.; Rammelkamp, 1928, pp. 383–384; Sweet, 1937, pp. 153–154; Norton, 1895, p. 24.

Despite the high praise heaped on the new system, few institutions adopted it without qualification. Some requirements remained in a multitude of compromises with the traditional curriculum, attained in practice by mediating among the claims of contending departments. But there was also an earnest and persistent effort to justify the college program. A conviction survived that the subjects on each degree recipient's record ought to reflect some common definition of the culture bestowed upon him. Schemes for majors and minors sought to give order to the choices, and devices for distribution aimed to guarantee that "no window into the scientific 'palace of delight'" was "darkened for the man of culture."[24]

At Chicago, Cornell, and occasionally elsewhere some faculty members believed that the "ideal institution of learning, so far as the word *home* is concerned" was Oxford, where daily social intercourse between teachers and students provided an enviable context for instruction. Imitation was not feasible, however, because the costs were high, and also because the dominant tendency of American educational development set the social and the academic aspects of college in separate, though related, categories. And despite occasional complaints about the lecture system, most students preferred it that way; they insisted on respect "of the fine line that separates instructor from instructed, on whose side neither may trespass" and resented intrusions by older men seeking to recapture a lost youth. The boys also accepted the fact that knowledge was divided into segments called courses, a quota of which was the price of four years of relative freedom. Tutoring schools and purchased "trots" or "ponies" eased the boredom or pain of compulsory attendance at class and of prescribed reading and examinations. Meanwhile the undergraduate with genuine intellectual interests could browse where he wished with a loose tether. The one building of a prairie college was a beacon light to the farm boy whose only preparation had been from an old one-eyed man who taught a little arithmetic and grammar in an abandoned store building; and the immigrant youth who fought his way up from the dense public high school found not only opportunity but also cultural liberation in the university.[25]

---

[24] Sloane, 1895, pp. 121–122; Hadley, 1895, p. 64; McCosh, 1878, p. 435; Collins, 1914, p. 227; Gavit, 1925, p. 27.

[25] Storr, 1966, pp. 322–323, 326–327; Bishop, 1962, p. 333; Dartmouth College, 1924, p. 24; Flandrau, 1897, pp. 265ff., 269, 279, 291ff.; Angell, 1928, p. 3; Benn, 1928, p. 79ff.; Santayana, 1934, p. 57; Geiger, 1958, p. 36; Blackorby, 1963, pp. 8–9.

The freedom of the faculty members was qualified by the expectation that they display in their lives and work the attributes of character and scholarship instructive to their charges. On every campus there were professors who won popularity by their eccentricities or performing skills. But most of their colleagues played more modest roles. As institutions grew in size and complexity, burgeoning administrative staffs overshadowed the professor who sometimes seemed a less consequential figure than the football coach. Probably no college was free of the burble of subterranean resentments which sprang from jealousies, disappointments, restraints upon personal life, and poverty. Occasional demands for an improvement of status, however, were not loudly voiced, for those who adopted the vocation of professor did so either out of the love of scholarship or the desire to teach and were willing to forgo any other function in return for the liberty to do what they wished. The "Ph.D. octopus" or "doctor monopoly" which William James feared was far from having conquered the campus even in 1930. Nor did the myth of "publish or perish" ever damage good teaching—whatever that was. But the devotion to scholarship was an ideal of commanding attractiveness, even to those who never themselves attained it. The sense of professional solidarity that united professors everywhere gave all a share in the esteem accorded the few creative or influential figures.[26]

The prestige of scholarship also earned the "prof" the respect, or at least the tolerance of the undergraduates, so that he became part of the good old days later to be recalled with affection and amusement. The tricks of the past, such as locking an instructor in his room or "throwing water upon him, stealing his clothes or other property, upsetting his chair in recitation or tripping him up outside" were now disdained "not because they could not be played with perfect impunity, but because the general college sentiment condemns them as unmanly and indecent." The faculty were like clergymen without a church, woodenly sober and slim as their pay, droning away about some forgotten truth but maintaining the standards of virtue and honor in a money-getting nation. Their willingness to devote themselves to the truth which made them "content with less remuneration than can be obtained in ordinary business" was evidence of their disinterested defense of the modern community against its own material prosperity. Men who pursued "their studies primarily for the sake of pure

[26] Jastrow, 1912, p. 496ff.; Christensen, 1912, p. 11; Paton, 1911; McGrath, 1938; Bishop, 1962, p. 355; James, 1903, pp. 1–9; Storr, 1966, pp. 308–309.

learning, and not for a livelihood" were the appropriate custodians of the nation's culture and of its youth.[27]

The quasi-monastic ideal exacted its toll from the professors and their families. But it also shifted emphasis away from transmission of a common body of doctrine in favor of "the impartial assemblage and mutual confrontation of all sorts of ideas," which in turn "produced in intellectual matters, a sort of happy watchfulness and insecurity." The university could be trusted to extend an "open-handed hospitality to all truth," said Andrew Lipscomb when the Methodists opened Vanderbilt in 1875, because it rested on the "unity of a scholarly temper." In a characteristic American compromise, scholarship did not seem incongruous with, but rather conducive to, the environment for the production of a college man (Fisher, 1915, p. 15ff.; Santayana, 1934, p. 163; Mims, 1946, p. 64).

**VARIATIONS OF THE COLLEGE THEME**   The identical conception of the social function of schools for the age group between 18 and 22 penetrated even among groups which could not quite attain the distinction of the college man. People whose access to higher education was limited by discrimination or exclusion formed institutions of their own, which they nevertheless shaped to an image similar to that already in existence.

No woman could quite become a college man. True, there was a rapid spread of coeducation and, to the extent that teaching became a female career, it made sense to afford girls the opportunity to equip themselves for that vocation. Nor was there any question of their competence to perform the required academic tasks. Nevertheless, the impression of inadequacy persisted and produced an array of associated or separate colleges, for which there was no European counterpart (Bishop, 1962, p. 143ff.; Curti & Carstensen, I, 1949, p. 193).

Scholarly women, such as Maria Mitchell and Martha Carey Thomas, regarded the development as inevitable but regrettable. Segregation was occasionally justified by the need for special instruction in hygiene or physiology, and it had the virtue of finding places for female teachers to whom doors were still closed elsewhere. But the primary impulse was the desire "to strengthen the

[27] Bagg, 1871, pp. 657–658; Santayana, 1934, p. 43ff.; Canby, 1915, p. 4; Kelly, 1926, p. 16; *Addresses, Inauguration of Eliot,* 1869, p. 48; Aurner, 1916, p. 48; Rogers, 1942, p. 147; Bowman, 1938, p. 54; Norton, 1895, p. 32; Morison, 1936b, pp. 402–403.

social and physical life of the men and women on different lines."
The considerations that swayed girls in the choice of a college were
not unlike those that influenced boys; courses and professors were
less important than the fact that their high school chums were in
Pi Omega or Pi Delta. Yet young ladies could not be full and equal
participants in coeducational activities or studies and were generally shunted to secondary roles even in literary and cultural
organizations. In the arrangement of the social calendar and in
joint affairs the sororities were doomed to follow the lead of the
fraternities. Smith, Wellesley, Radcliffe, and Barnard, each, though
in different ways, aimed to break that pattern of dependence.[28]

Central to all these efforts was the recognition that the college
involved relationships that were not purely academic and that
therefore had to provide a distinctive place for women. The round
of activities in the separate or coordinated institutions, as indeed,
in the coeducational ones, as far as possible attempted to provide
an equivalent for the social life normal to the college man. Girls,
like boys, had a right to the "unequaled opportunities" college
life offered "merely for good times, for romance, for society"
(Palmer, 1899, p. 51; Angell, 1928, p. 141ff.).

Negroes suffered from total or partial exclusion despite emanci-
pation. In the decades after the Civil War, a trickle of colored
young men and women passed through the prestigious colleges
and universities of the North, especially where an abolitionist influence persisted. Admission requirements then were not restrictive
and the number of qualified applicants was not so large as to present a problem. But in the South, where the great majority of
freedmen still lived and where the level of preparation for whites
and blacks was low, there seemed little hope that existing institutions of higher education would provide opportunities for Negroes.
The establishment of segregation by law extinguished any expectation that the situation might change for the better. And
after the turn of the century, the spread of racist doctrines north-
ward actually lessened the prospects of Negroes for higher education. The result was the development of a system of separate
colleges, some private, others created by the states in order to preserve the lily-white character of existing institutions. Starved for
funds, the colored colleges labored under heartbreaking difficulties.

[28] Bishop, 1962, pp. 337–338, 347; Montross, 1923, p. 204ff.; Storr, 1966, p.
324; Millis, 1927, p. 235ff.

Measured by the usual academic standards, the results of these efforts were meager; yet there were generally no other means of further education for the ill-prepared, poverty-stricken products of segregated elementary and secondary schools.[29]

Negro students, whether segregated or not, aspired to emulate the model of the college man. The pathos of the experience of the first colored cadet at West Point arose from his eagerness to conform and his willingness to accept the code. The boys admitted to prestigious schools lived, insofar as they could, the life of other students and emerged loyal alumni. Within the Negro colleges, there was a pervasive effort to follow the curricular and extracurricular activity accepted as normal in the United States.[30]

Catholics, unlike women or Negroes, met no such formal barriers to admission to any college. Indeed, their presence was rather welcome, even in sectarian institutions, as a means of converting or Americanizing the members of what many still regarded as a foreign faith. Catholic students, however, were not fully accepted in college life, for they failed to meet the test—"Would you want your sister to marry one?" Exclusion by some fraternities and social clubs created tension and no doubt left many young men smarting with bitter resentments. Furthermore, parents and students and their pastors suspected that the secular university, and certainly the sectarian one, was a menace to faith; and some Catholic separateness in social life was a self-imposed safeguard against that danger (Whalen, 1964, p. 25ff.; Cross, 1950, p. 133ff.).

The fears, both of rejection and conversion, encouraged the spread of a Catholic system of higher education which increasingly aimed not only to recruit potential seminarians but also to supply an acceptable environment for the lay leaders of the future. Operating under the supervision of the clergy, these colleges could teach without departing from orthodox doctrine and could also train the young men and women who passed through them in the behavior appropriate to their faith (Power, 1958, p. 203ff.).

Nevertheless, the influence of the common American collegiate model exerted steady pressure upon the Catholic schools. The

[29] McMillan, 1952; Bullock, 1967, pp. 66ff., 123ff.; Holmes, 1934; Caliver, 1928, p. 6ff.

[30] Campbell, 1936, p. 47ff.; Flipper, 1878; Broderick, p. 22ff.; Bullock, 1967, p. 166ff. There is an account of William Henry Lewis in the *Boston Herald,* Jan. 2, 1948.

authority of science raised disturbing problems of modernism and Americanism. There was a gradual shift to the elective system. Student life, in social organization, residences, intercollegiate athletics and fashions of behavior acquired features remarkably similar to those of the secular universities (Cross, 1950, p. 146ff.).

**COLLEGIATE UNREST**  Inevitably there were strains in a system which drew together scholars, presumably intent upon the pursuit of knowledge, and students without a clear sense of purpose preparing to prepare for careers. That it functioned at all was due to mutual tolerance and to the willingness to leave unreconciled the contradictory elements in the system. But the tensions also led to frequent outbreaks of disorder, and riots regularly punctuated the college year (Curti & Carstensen, I, 1949, p. 550ff.).

These difficulties reached a crescendo in the decade after the end of the First World War. Albion in Michigan and St. Stephen's in New York rebelled against their presidents; protests against military training at Ohio State, against compulsory chapel at Oberlin, and against physical education at Howard led to major crises; and the *Harvard Crimson* launched an anti-football campaign. Underground student newspapers — *Gadfly* at Harvard, *Critic* at Oberlin, *Proletarian* at Wisconsin, *Saturday Evening Pest* at Yale, and *Tempest* at Michigan — demanded not only the right to ask critical questions but also the right to give the answers. The call for the privilege of shaping their own curriculum became part of the program of the National Federation of American Students founded in 1925. Trustees and administrators, suspicious of their faculties, sympathetic to the boys-will-be-boys students, and anxious to avoid unfavorable publicity, were "easily frightened by mass actions" and disposed to buy off the young. Experiment became fashionable: Antioch revived the work-study idea; Alexander Meiklejohn went to Wisconsin to launch an altogether new kind of college; Brookwood in New York and Commonwealth in Arkansas were to serve labor; and undergraduates formed a free-floating Student University in Connecticut.[31]

There was agitation among the faculties also — not the long-standing discontent with restrictive routine which had always troubled scholars like William James, but rather irritation about power, status and salary. The immense stadia and unions were

[31] Kirkpatrick, 1926, pp. 204–209, 211–215, 222, 226–239; Henderson & Hall, 1946; Meiklejohn, 1928; Feuer, 1969, p. 344; Bishop, 1962, p. 488ff.

annoying reminders of the disparity between the resources devoted to students and those available to teachers. Academic unrest in Germany and England had stirred ripples of interest across the Atlantic; Americans who knew about the protests of assistant professors and docents and about the proposals for reform by Lord Curzon and Tillgard were less disposed to docility than formerly. The threat to academic freedom during and after the war and the much publicized cases of Beard and Cattell were a stimulus to organization and the assertion of rights. Even the Soviet revolution was regarded as an omen of the democratization of the universities. One reformer in all innocence expressed the hope that self-government, including the participation of students in faculty meetings, "may be a common practice in America as it is to-day in Russia."[32]

Furthermore, some of the contradictions implicit in higher education came to the surface in the 1920s. It was desirable to have all freshmen live in the same dormitories, but it was not fair to force a white to share his room with a Negro; better to provide otherwise for colored students! Some colleges could no longer admit every applicant and yet were unwilling to adopt a single standard for the selection of the future leaders of society; better to set quotas for Jews and other alien types who might not fit fully into the whole life of the institution! Awkward controversies followed (*New York Times,* Jan. 12, 1923, p. 5).

The rumblings from within were threatening because they exposed the university to attack from external foes. Muckrakers criticized it as "an instrument of special privilege" designed "to keep America capitalist." Carry Nation and other zealots exposed it as a den of iniquity; after a local minister alleged that 2,000 whores battened on the boys in New Haven, a detective sent privately to investigate conditions at Harvard discovered details "too disgusting to be published," but fully as bad as those at Yale. Harried deans struggled to maintain order, to appease their charges, and yet to satisfy the ferocious alumni who insisted, "this new license and socialistic rant, the mental and moral bounders, must be held down."[33]

The university suffered in the 1920s because of "the world-wide lapse from culture." The postwar breakdown of the European

[32] Allen, 1967, p. 341ff.; Benn, 1928, p. 63; Hall, 1923, p. 342ff.; Kirkpatrick, 1926, pp. 295–296.

[33] Sinclair, 1922, p. 18; Nation, 1909, p. 249ff.; Crane, 1909, p. 128; Benn, 1928, p. 88; Hergesheimer, 1922, p. 139.

sources of authority to which Americans had formerly appealed for support and, at the same time, the widespread questioning within the United States of accepted canons in the sciences, philosophy, the arts, and literature undermined the role of the college as transmitter of durable values, tastes, beliefs, and traditions. Nor could the training in the genteel manners hold much attraction at a time when aristocrats of ancient lineage were in exile or in debt and when the children of the putative moneyed aristocracy showed no interest in their parents' aspirations (Hall, 1923, p. 516).

Rebellion therefore became a conventional student posture. Intellectually, it took the form of a call for liberation "from the entanglement of mere traditional authority and provincial prejudice" and for the discard of the millstones of "dead formalism in religion, and narrow thinking in social relations." The demands were peremptory: "Saccharine Sunday-school religion, blatant Fourth-of-July Patriotism, inherited class bias—all must fall." A pronounced shift in patterns of personal behavior expressed the same impatience with institutional restraints. The lost generation—self-proclaimed—flaunted its interest in sex and whiskey in defiance of the Puritans and of the prohibition laws and provided a compelling model for college youth. "The modernity of jazz and jungle dancing, of raw styles and rouge, of novels and frankness and unashamed sex" troubled the Dean of Women. "She knew positively that they were not dancing six inches apart in obedience to the edict she had issued when the shimmy dances had come straight from the black and tan cabarets of Chicago to the hectic sex-swirl that was the State University." Yet by the 1920s the automobile had brought unprecedented freedom, for it liberated joy-riding youngsters from whatever restraints still operated within the campus and the town. Whether the defiance of the old code was confined to words and daydreams or was extended into action, the campus beauty queens and flask-toting men of the postwar decade followed a standard rather different from that of the genteel culture formerly entrusted to the custody of the college.[34]

In 1930, there was no expectation that the college would be able to control behavior or draw young people back to the old code, for it had long since become reconciled to the autonomy of student life within very broad limits. It exerted influence only through the

[34] Dartmouth College, 1924, p. 13; Montross, 1923, p. 186; Benn, 1928, p. 94ff.; Angell, 1928, pp. 7, 167ff.; Kinsey, 1948; Kinsey, 1953.

creation of an environment of culture within which the students were to find the proper guidelines. If they were unable or unwilling to do so, or if there were doubts about the guidelines themselves, then educators would have to reexamine the purpose of the four years thus expended, a task few wished to undertake.

The bold promoters of the 1870s had hoped to end an earlier uncertainty about purpose by shifting the orientation of higher education from traditional religion to scientific knowledge. For a time, faith in a unifying culture reaching out to the whole society through its future leaders had made feasible an improbable junction between the socializing function of the college and the scholarly activities of the university. With that faith weakened, the institutions of higher learning in the United States, despite their wealth and numbers, were unprepared for the crises of the next three decades.

# 5. The Discipline of Scholarship, 1930–1960

In the history of the American university the three decades after 1930 were full of paradoxes. The consistent developments perceptible in retrospect were not evident from year to year, so that events appeared to unfold erratically in response to unpredictable impulses; and often what seemed to be a move in one direction proved in reality an adjustment in course toward quite a different destination. Through much of this period, educators, trustees, and legislators took a gloomy view of the future of higher education; nevertheless, the institutions grew in number, in size, and even in wealth and in power. The count rose from 1,409 in 1930 to 1,850 in 1957, and enrollments more than doubled, from 1,101,000 to 2,637,000; in 1960, enrollment stood at 3,500,000. Yet the expansion came without preparation, almost without awareness (Bureau of Census, 1957, pp. 210–211; U.S. Office of Education, 1960, Part 3).

It was difficult to distinguish long-term from short-term trends. The period began with a decade of worldwide depression, which led into a long era of active and cold war. Both depression and war had cataclysmic effects on the universities. However, neither was to exert as deep an influence on the university as other changes that altered the situation of youth in the economy and in the society.

Despite the unemployment of the 1930s, this proved to be a time of sustained economic growth. Output returned to its prosperity levels by 1937 and was further stimulated by the war. The postwar depression that many observers anticipated in 1945 failed to materialize. Instead, growth continued through the 1950s, although at varying rates. Expansion, involving as it did technological innovation at every stage of production and distribution, favored large, impersonally organized corporate enterprise. During the years between 1930 and 1960 there was a consistent increase in the size of the bureaucracy at all levels of government and in many nonpolitical agencies, including those devoted to health, social welfare, and education. By contrast, the numbers occupied in agriculture and in the handicrafts declined.

After 1930, still more than earlier, it was clear that opportunity lay not in independent entrepreneurship but rather in the access to strategic places on the steps upward within a large organization. Only medicine still emphasized the individual practitioner; the other professions, including business, were more formally structured than previously. Furthermore, the increasing emphasis upon technology and the extension of mechanization enhanced the value of advanced training. It seemed plausible to continue the earlier tendency toward making all skills available through instruction in institutions of higher education.

Moreover, young people between the ages of 18 and 22 were less and less likely to discover alternative modes of launching a desirable career. The depression was particularly hard upon job-seeking youth, and when the end of the war relieved the acute manpower shortage, the casual employments that had once provided stepping stones for some tended to disappear: bureaucratic organizations required credentials of those they hired; unions set tight requirements around valuable positions; and mechanization eased the need for hands. The high school graduate, unwanted on the labor market, had a desperate need for the college degree; and the number of families that could afford to assist their children to that goal rose with the general increase of incomes.

As a result, college attendance climbed despite the declining birth rates of the 1920s and 1930s, which supplied the cohorts of the postwar years. The rise in the number of births after 1940 would add further to the college population 20 years later. But the increase in the number of students was already well under way before the products of the baby boom matured. Until 1960, the increment was due not so much to an expansion of the eligible age group as to a rise in the percentage of those who chose to continue their education beyond the high school level (President's Commission, I, 1947, p. 25, II, p. 40).

The insistence of an increasing proportion of young people between 18 and 22 upon a period in college was due in part to the economic value ascribed to the degree and, in part, to the failure of society to make alternative provision for this age group. But the widespread expectation of a college experience owed something also to the growing egalitarianism of the period after 1930. The universities were no longer to be "merely the instrument for producing an intellectual elite," insisted a presidential commission in 1947. They were to "become the means by which every citizen, youth and adult, is enabled and encouraged to carry his education, formal and informal, as far as his native capacities permit." The ideal had sources deep in the nineteenth century; and the Depression, the New Deal, the war, and the general reaction against aristocratic values strengthened it. The society which assumed responsibility for aiding each individual to become self-supporting could hardly evade the obligation to help young people along the steps necessary to establish them in careers. This was the philosophy of the G.I. Bill, as a result of which the federal government was supplying one-third of the operating revenue of institutions of higher education in 1947. By 1960, the same view had gained a general, though imprecise currency: every American had a right to higher education, along with life, liberty, and the other means of pursuing happiness (President's Commission, I, 1947, p. 101, V, p. 53ff.)

Associated with the aspiration of opening the colleges to all was the assurance, also traditionally sanctified in academic oratory and in appeals for funds, that the university would supply the formulas for solving society's problems, that it would perform as a "service station for the general public." To discharge its obligations, it needed scholars with "a passionate concern for human betterment, for the improvement of social conditions, and of relations among men." Such educators would "apply at the point of social action what the social scientist has discovered regarding the laws of human behavior." The colleges were to "become laboratories of inter-race and interfaith fellowship" by eliminating all forms of discrimination. For every student they would "offset the handicaps of secondary school instruction which is of poor quality." And they would undertake massive programs of adult education (Wilson, 1942, p. 175; President's Commission, I, 1947, pp. 30–32, 37, 91, 101, II, pp. 26–27, 36–38, 41ff., III, p. 7).

**POSTWAR BOOM** These unexceptionable sentiments did not take account of the actualities of the academic situation and therefore complicated the efforts of the universities to absorb the shock of massive growth. To begin with, American colleges had been set for contraction and retrenchment, partly as a result of the Depression, partly as a consequence of the misreading of the potential market for graduates and the fear of turning loose a mass of unemployed degree-holders as Germany had after the First World War. In consequence, administrators and professors alike consistently underestimated the dimensions of future expansion (Harris, 1949; President's Commission, I, 1947, p. 39).

Furthermore, the rhetoric, no matter how benevolent the intentions, did not bridge the gap between social and academic reality. The social reality was the existence of a large and growing age group which had no function but attendance at some kind of school. The academic reality was the existence of colleges increasingly staffed by scholars primarily concerned with an array of specialized disciplines.

The presidential commission of 1947 estimated that to meet the increase it foresaw by 1960, colleges would have to add 250,000 new teachers to their faculties. The whole number of doctorates produced in the 1930s was 20,783; of these degree-holders some 65 percent went on to teach. The commission therefore recommended a speedup of preparation, with less emphasis on research and more on techniques of instruction. Of course, it also counseled the graduate schools to put training in the hands of "men of broad knowledge, men of imagination and understanding, and wisdom" (President's Commission, I, 1947, pp. 87–89, IV, p. 27; Hofstadter & Hardy, 1952, p. 67).

Not a professor in the country but would have recognized in those phrases an accurate appraisal of his own qualifications! The faculties, having steadily and successfully fought for recognition of their professional status, brought an exhilarating sense of confidence—even of arrogance—to their work. In occasional small rural colleges, the teacher still cowered beneath the tyranny of president, trustees, and community. But that situation was becoming ever less usual: the struggles of the American Association of University Professors since 1915 had won recognition of the principles of tenure; and violations of academic freedom, even during the Depression and the McCarthy period, were gratifyingly few (Lazarsfeld & Thielens, 1958).

Moreover, professors had been gaining in popular esteem. Access to their ranks was difficult and therefore of itself a sign of competence. And their abilities, while specialized, were not confined to abstract matters. Practical men of affairs had run the country into a depression; the brain trust and its successors, consulted by government and by business, controlled the knowledge that could save the nation. War service confirmed that impression. The value set upon research grew rapidly; and the foundations, which had already begun to operate earlier in the century, increasingly supplied support that relieved scholars of total dependence upon the college budget, despite some initial resistance from the universities. Indeed, institutions of higher education often had to compete for personnel against industry and government. True, salaries remained low by significant criteria. Nevertheless, the scholar after 1930 achieved a good deal of autonomy, and even critics who measured performance by the yardstick of utility recognized that the universities should concentrate on basic research rather than "turning themselves into institutes of applied science."[1]

The faculty in this period won almost complete power over teaching appointments. Budgetary restraints remained, as did the formal veto of administrators and trustees. But a large and growing percentage of appointments were by the co-option of the professors themselves, according to the internal standards of their discipline. The infusion of refugees from communist and fascist regimes in Europe helped diminish parochialism. Discrimination against ethnic and cultural outsiders subsided, and it became inappropriate to scrutinize the details of character, attitudes, values, and personal life that had once been weighty elements in the designation to a teaching position. The only relevant question was the extent to which the instructor had mastered his body of knowledge and the only relevant answer was that derived from scrutiny of his degrees, publications, and other credentials. The fact that he would also be a teacher of the youth under his charge was secondary in the appointment process as it was in graduate training (Berelson, 1960; President's Commission, IV, 1947, p. 6).

The growing importance in the college of science, that is, of the organized body of knowledge, gave control over the most weighty decisions to the departments which were the institutional projections of the disciplines of scholarship. Knowledge itself having become complex and specialized, it was no longer possible to assume that all the members of a faculty would have the competence to understand or judge each other's work. The proliferating departments corresponded to the growing fragmentation of scholarship.

This academic structure, whatever its utility in advancing re-

[1] Keppel, 1930, p. 29; President's Commission, I, 1947, pp. 92–94; Caplow & McGee, 1959; Jones, Riesman, & Ulich, 1962, pp. 21ff., 37ff.; Hofstadter & Hardy, 1952, p. 57.

search, was not on the face of it a plausible device for administering education to the host of students who came to college, not to master any discipline, but, in some imprecise sense, to span the years between adolescence and adulthood. Yet for a time at least, the autonomous faculty, divided into departments, proved surprisingly effective, not because it could execute fully the mission society now assigned to it, nor because of the special merit of the curricula over which it wrangled, but rather because professors enjoyed an environment of freedom in which they could pursue their scholarship and in which they commanded the respect of the young people who grew up in their proximity.

**CURRICULUM REFORMS**
But the broad visions of its future role disoriented the university. The mandate to encourage every citizen to carry his education as far as his native capacities permitted was ambiguous. It could be interpreted with emphasis on opportunity: the college was then a sieve, applying rigid standards to all who passed through it and sorting them out according to ability. Or, it could be interpreted in terms of common if not identical experience: all Americans aged 18 to 22 were entitled to their college years, in which case it would be necessary "to provide a much greater variety of institutions and programs than we now have" in order to accommodate varying aptitudes (President's Commission, I, 1947, p. 41).

Given this ambiguity, no ready formula was at hand for what to teach or how to occupy the vast body of young people who now moved into the colleges. The disarray of society gradually emptied of meaning the whole notion of preparation for a gentlemanly style of life, particularly since attendance became so general as to lose the cachet of exclusiveness. The conception of an established genteel culture, already in dissolution before 1930, died with the Depression and with the victory of the avant-garde in the arts and even in science, to be replaced by painful uncertainties and an open, questioning attitude toward the old verities. The willingness to experiment was therefore not confined to new institutions like Bard and Bennington. Nor was it merely fashionable; it reflected a genuine dissatisfaction both with the curriculum and the old pattern of college life.

The scholars within each department took an internal view of their subject, which they pressed upon the faculty as a whole in the usual juggling and balancing operations of university politics. The result was to turn the curriculum into a congeries of departmental courses, each taught by a specialist and linked by a variety of schemes which combined elements of compulsion and free election, of concentration and distribution (Brown, 1940). But however the elements were manipulated, no formal device could offset the subtle change in the character of the faculty, the members of which had ceased to be custodians of a general culture which they imparted to the youth under their supervision, and had become instead guardians of particular segments of knowledge that they expected to develop and spread.

There was consequently a circular quality to the recurrent efforts at reform, as earnest educators shifted about the same intractable materials available to them, just as their predecessors had for more than a century. Since it was easier to launch a new experiment than to appraise the results of an old one, the repetitious quality of the innovations was not surprising.

The hope of easing the task of devising a curriculum lay behind some of the efforts to arrange a preliminary differentiation among the students. The encouragement given the development of junior and community colleges derived to some extent from the expectation that they would divert less prepared or less interested students away from the senior institutions. But since no one wished to close the doors to further education, it was clear that the two-year college, which offered "a well-integrated single program" that was both "general and vocational," would also prepare some to go on for two years more (President's Commission, III, 1947, p. 5ff.).

The full-fledged college flatly rejected the suggestion of a pass degree after the English style; every baccalaureate was to be earned, somehow. But it was another matter to set some unprepared or unmotivated students apart in a general college in order to disencumber others of their presence. Nor did it seem invidious to devote special attention to the ablest in honors programs, as Swarthmore had since 1922. The lecture, while still the preponderant teaching technique in most colleges, seemed inappropriate for the best students. Even before 1930, there had been experiments — tutorial and the house system at Harvard, preceptorial at Princeton — aimed at establishing intimacy with the instructors, and the projects directed at the same end multiplied in the decades that followed. The desire to devote special attention to the brainiest culminated in the 1950s in a widespread hunt for excellence — as if that were a discrete, definable attribute. The surge of applicants for admission in that decade permitted the most prestigious institutions to raise requirements and, in effect, to devote themselves to a select group of undergraduates (Spafford, 1943; Aydelotte, 1944; Hofstadter & Hardy, 1952, p. 115ff.).

But numbers had a way of catching up with the elite programs. Now, as for more than a century in American education, the pressure to make distinction available to all ran only a little behind the pressure to admit everyone; and only the financially secure private institutions could resist. Those who argued for a wider view charged that "the present orientation of higher education toward verbal skills and intellectual interests" was too restrictive, and, by implication at least, they demanded accommodations for the unskilled and unintellectual. The university had to provide enough variety so that everyone could do well in something. The number of new course offerings therefore continued to mount at an accelerating pace, in a process that seemed to conform to the elaboration and fragmentation of scholarship (President's Commission, I, 1947, p. 32).

The remorseless thickening of the course catalog dismayed even the proponents of diversification. The same report which counseled the colleges to avoid excessive orientation to intellectual interests, went on to complain that "the unity of liberal education has been splintered by overspecialization."

What was to be done? The question had reechoed through the decades since the abandonment of the classical curriculum. "Some community of values, ideas, and attitudes" appeared "essential as a cohesive force in this age of minute division of labor and intense conflict of special interests." The cluster of survey courses, which in most places constituted the required elements in the degree program, were not adequate to the task of transmitting a liberal education to the heterogeneous body of students now passing through the college (President's Commission, I, 1947, pp. 47, 49).

The drawbacks of the elective system, even when balanced by set requirements, were evident enough to stimulate interest in new offerings aimed directly and specifically at general as against specialized education. In 1919, Columbia had devised a course on contemporary civilization out of which grew a program intended to define the "intellectual and spiritual tradition that a man must experience and understand if he is to be called educated." The College at the University of Chicago made a still more ambitious effort to structure undergraduate teaching so that it would be unfettered by the boundaries of conventional departments and disciplines. The adoption of a program in general education at Harvard in 1945 signaled the apparent victory of this approach (Miner, 1954, p. 47; Harvard University, 1945).

President Robert M. Hutchins' talent for pushing a good idea to absurdity exposed the limitations of general education. The core of the curriculum, he announced, was "the same at any time, in any place, under any political, social, or economic conditions"—a dictum which could be applied to a handful of students at St. John's or could promote the great books publishing venture, but was inapplicable to American youth in their vast diversity. Actually, compromise everywhere began to alter these programs almost as soon as they were formulated. In some institutions, general education became an alternative to scholarship, both as a route to a teaching career and as a repository for "spiritual content" to offset the harsh scientism of the departments. Elsewhere, the old departmental surveys simply acquired new titles, numbers, and budgets. But the most durable and most common effect was unforeseen.

General education offerings absolved the remainder of the curriculum of the obligation of taking account of undergraduates. Faculties which voted in the new programs in effect created, or recognized, a dichotomy between general and specialized courses. The consequences of thus widening the distance between most of the students and most of the scholars would not become apparent until after 1960 (Hutchins, 1936, pp. 66–67; Hofstadter & Hardy, 1952, p. 55ff.).

Indeed, through much of this period there was a conscious effort to pull student and teacher together by involving each in the interests of the other. The expansion of the catalog made possible formal instruction in areas previously left to voluntary effort. Undergraduate organizations had always drawn upon the advice of interested faculty members. But the incorporation of music, the drama, journalism, and athletics into the pattern of course offerings had the effect of attenuating the distinction between curricular and extracurricular affairs. The tendency was general, although rarely recognized as openly or as boldly as at Bennington (Jones, 1946).

The personal associations thus created undoubtedly proved rewarding to those involved. But the side effects were ultimately costly. As one activity after another was officially assimilated into the catalog and the academic framework, the area within which undergraduates were left alone to manage matters in their own way, by themselves, narrowed. At the same time, the students learned to depend upon the formal university structure for the whole of their college experience rather than, as earlier, for only a part, and not always the most important part, of it. It became difficult for a young man or woman to conceive of reading a book or playing the cymbals or making a movie without somehow receiving credit for it. The reckoning of gains and losses from the change would not come until after 1960 when students, having become totally dependent upon the curriculum, naturally found themselves dissatisfied with it.

**THE CHANGING STUDENT BODY** Despite the glaring contradictions in its character, the university thrived and, between 1930 and 1960, experienced less difficulty in managing its students than in any period of the same duration, either before or since then. The times were uncertain, and the juxtaposition of scholarship with the mass of young people without clear aims left the curriculum disorderly and blurred the purposes of the institution. Still, the very lack of precise definition created an environment in which all the participants in the college enterprise had remarkable freedom to do what they wished.

For the time being, the coexistence of scholars and students proved possible. Notwithstanding the denigration long directed at the Ph.D. and its related paraphernalia, the degree proved a useful device for staffing the faculties, so long as the numbers involved were relatively low, for a network of personal communication within the disciplines permitted an appraisal of individuals that went beyond the paper credentials. Not every college teacher held the degree and not every holder of the degree was a creative scholar; but enough were to establish the norm and to commit the institutions in which they functioned to the pursuit of knowledge, to objectivity, and to rational procedures in the use of evidence. There were enough also to endow the faculty as a whole with prestige that commanded the respect of the students.

The consciousness of participation in a respected enterprise, in addition, had a stimulating effect upon many worthy teachers who had allowed the aspirations toward original scholarship to lapse, but who were sustained by a sense of participation in the transmission, if not the advance, of learning. Numbers had not yet grown so large as to destroy the unity of a department or professional meeting, despite the inevitable clashes of personality and points of view. Moreover, the rapid expansion of specialized personnel for guidance, religious, psychiatric, and health services relieved the faculty of tasks which had once been incidental to teaching and at the same time interposed a variety of shock absorbers between professors and students (President's Commission, II, 1947, p. 43; Miner, 1954, p. 66).

Above all, the changing composition of the student body eased the problems of dealing with it. Drawn from a wider segment of the whole society than previously, it lacked the common assumptions basic to earlier college life, was more susceptible to the influence of such external events as war and depression, and was, therefore, more serious about its studies. The prospects of few families were so secure, even in the 1950s, that their offspring could afford to ignore the problems of finding a career. And the rising percentage of young students whose parents had incomes below the national median produced a general consciousness of the need for using the years of study to lay a basis for future security. The return of the veterans brought to the campus older, more mature students, many of them married and burdened with family obligations of their own; they had lost time in life, had experienced much, and were totally in earnest about what they were doing. In fact, for such people the tensions of college life were likely to arise out of the competitive desire for getting ahead (Sanford, 1962; Handlin, 1951, p. 25ff.; 1962, p. 41ff.).

The focus of student concern upon performance in accredited courses and of faculty concern upon scholarship altered the disciplinary relationship. What happened outside the classroom lost importance. The remaining supervisory aspects of the college now decayed almost to the vanishing point. Compulsory chapel slipped into gentle desuetude, despite the renewal of interest in religion in the 1950s and the rising membership of Newman, Hillel, and other voluntary church-oriented organizations. The regulation of personal behavior grew lax, and while the rules sometimes remained unchanged, they were rarely enforced in the absence of public scandal or internal conflict. The student increasingly was conceded autonomy and was expected to guide his conduct in his own way. The college's residual right to exercise oversight over its charges, while not surrendered, was invoked reluctantly and infrequently (Feuer, 1969, p. 375ff.).

It was symptomatic that the fraternities and other societies which had formerly been so central to the college experience lost much of their importance. Some were tainted by discriminatory and exclusionary practices out of accord with the egalitarianism of the period. Furthermore, the blurring of the distinction between curricular and extracurricular affairs shifted undergraduate interest to activities conducted under college auspices, especially where there was an official effort to draw the whole student body together in unions or in such residential and instructional units as the Harvard and Yale houses. The fraternities which held on did so through inertia, the shortage of alternative living space, the uncertainty about how to change, and the interest of alumni.

An attrition also occurred in many related college customs—in hazing, in initiation rituals, and in distinctive requirements of dress—which students had formerly imposed upon themselves. There was no end to spontaneous pranks and to the maniacal outbursts of swallowing goldfish or crowding into telephone booths. But the institutional patterns in which such impulses had earlier been channeled were in process of dissolution. There were signs that the passion was even draining out of intercollegiate athletics.

The spread of the belief among undergraduates that learning was the main business of college also inhibited the development of political activities. Unlike their counterparts in Europe and in Latin America, students in the United States did not become a political force of consequence. Clubs associated with the national parties occasionally used the labor of undergraduates in electoral campaigns and provided training for budding politicians. More radical organizations now and then attained a public notoriety unjustified by their meager numbers. The American Student Union, formed in 1935 by a merger, never attained the 12,000 members it claimed and became an easy front for the Communists, who also guided much of the anti-war movement before 1941. Such groups played a serious role on only a few exceptional campuses. Nor did their conservative counterparts of the 1950s gain significant ground.[2]

The reluctance of students to participate in radical movements sprang partly from the activity of the Communists, who on the one hand were devious, disruptive, and schismatic, and, on the other, rendered their fellow travelers vulnerable to charges of disloyalty that might prove damaging to future careers. But more important inner deterrents also inhibited any political involvements, radical

[2] Feuer, 1969, pp. 353ff., 361ff., 370ff.; Wechsler, 1935; Buckley, 1954; Evans, 1962.

or conservative. American college students were not homogeneous in social origins or in values and therefore lacked the common interests and attitudes that might provide a basis for national organization. Furthermore, it was rare in the United States to find men or women who stretched out their student status long enough to supply durable leadership or to provide continuity within the swiftly changing mass of those who passed through the university gates. Above all, for the overwhelming majority college was a transitional period rather than a career; undergraduates considered themselves transients on the way toward getting settled in life, and their main business was earning the degree. Hence their willingness to accept the discipline of scholarship, which, for the time being, permitted the university to encompass and serve a variety of dissimilar objectives.

Negro and Catholic institutions moved more slowly toward a relaxation of disciplinary controls because both types clung to an older view of the socialization function. Catholics still thought of the college as a bulwark to save the faith from the damaging effects of Americanization. Many influential Negroes continued to believe, out of "a gnawing need to preserve and foster" self-respect, that their own schools would develop the leadership of the future. Neither group therefore regarded integration as a wholly desirable goal; and both stressed the segregation of their colleges as an instrument for inculcating the unique values of their respective traditions. Discipline and the control of student life therefore remained tight. A visitor was astounded at "the lack of personal freedom that exists on most Negro campuses," which reminded him of mid-Victorian England. Not until after 1960 would Catholic and Negro institutions too feel the effects of the changes that had already transformed the socialization process in the majority of American colleges.[3]

By then, however, other forces were already undermining the trust in the capacity of knowledge, reflection, and reason to provide serious answers to the serious problems of life. Yet the belief in the validity of scholarship had been the silken band which loosely held the members of the university together. Without the authority thus voluntarily accepted, the diverse participants assembled in its numerous activities were in danger of flying apart; and the under-

[3] DuBois, 1933, p. 175; Buster, 1933, pp. 337–338; Hughes, 1933, p. 226; Bullock, 1967, pp. vii, 174.

graduates, now left with only the tenuous respect for scholarship as a source of discipline, were especially vulnerable.

**THE
EXPLOSIVE
SIXTIES**

Perhaps, 1957 would have made the logical terminal date for this study. That was the year of Sputnik, in reaction to which there followed many fateful alterations in the course of American higher education. But in retrospect that turning point seems not to have been as sharp as it appeared at the moment. The trends toward change were then already in existence, however little attention they attracted.

The massive infusion of federal funds into higher education after Sputnik had precedents, although it thereafter operated on a scale larger than before. Enrollments more than doubled between 1960 and 1969, rising to over 7 million in the latter year, responding to the rise of the birth rate two decades earlier, and to the weak position of youth in the labor market and in society, and to the effects of prosperity and federal aid upon the income constraints which had formerly blocked access to college. The subsequent strain upon a curriculum already in flux and upon student life already fragmented and disoriented was early evident (President's Commission, 1947, pp. 27–28, 39, 41; *Publishers' Weekly,* 1969, p. 33).

The consequences of expansion to the faculties might have been more difficult to forecast. The change in scale markedly diluted the quality and dignity of instruction everywhere; the means of preparing competent teachers in the necessary numbers were simply not available and the informal network of personal appraisal broke down, with nothing ready to replace it. As the rewards of the vocation increased, the motives for entering it became more complex than formerly, and the academic profession, which had long been on the defensive against any external criticism, suddenly discovered that it had internally neglected to define standards of responsibility, performance, or even malpractice. The result would severely test the assumption that expertise in a discipline alone was a sufficient criterion for the selection of teachers. Did a profound understanding of rocks or stars in itself qualify a man to deal with youth? Were the attributes of the professor as colleague, father, or husband which were relevant to his capacity to manage his personal affairs irrelevant to his capacity to manage students? Furthermore, deficiencies in the faculty were now less easily contained or concealed than formerly. The velocity of movement from job to job weakened the feeling of community among members of the same faculty or discipline; and the readiness to make place for out-siders—journalists, politicians, and bureaucrats from government and business—blurred the sense of the university as a unique institution dedicated to scholarly ends and values of its own.

Most difficult of all to anticipate were the alterations in the social environment. Education in the 1960s became a growth in-dustry, and the information business edged into the province that had formerly been monopolized by the library and the laboratory. Yet at the same time the university was still expected by society to provide a site for socializing an army of young people, most of whom were more familiar with the television screen than with the printed page and had been raised in utmost security by permissive parents. And the task had grown all the more difficult because a prosperous society immersed in sensation, easily swept by currents of irrationality, deeply puzzled by questions of national purpose, and uncertain about the content of the happiness it pursued was incapable of developing a consensus about the model toward which the young should be socialized.

Change was certainly not new to the American university, and often the impelling force had been the obligation to offer the young a preparation for entry to society. The first seminaries had not been able to confine themselves to their assigned task of raising a learned ministry, but assumed the additional responsibility of rearing young gentlemen according to religious and moral stan-dards. That concern had persisted on into the nineteenth century. Secularization and the assertion of the competence of science had not enabled the scholars to look inward upon their own problems, for the obligation to socialize the young lingered. Paradoxically, however, for three decades from 1930 to 1960, scholarship itself became the source of authority.

From generation to generation, however, through all these transformations, the university was also the home of men for whom learning—the pursuit of truth—was an end in itself and for whom the service of rearing the young was the price paid for the tolerance to pursue their own interests. A full history of the university might well balance the two elements; and in any estimate of future prospects, a significant question will certainly be the extent to which the obligation of socialization will remain compatible with scholarship.

# References

Adams, Charles K.: "The University of Michigan," in Charles F. Richardson and Henry A. Clark (eds.), *The College Book,* Osgood & Co., Boston, 1878.

Adams, Henry: *The Education of Henry Adams,* Riverside Press, Boston, 1918.

Adams, Herbert Baxter: *The College of William and Mary,* Government Printing Office, Washington, D.C., 1887.

*Addresses at the Inauguration of Charles William Eliot as President of Harvard College,* Cambridge, Mass., 1869.

Allen, Gay Wilson: *William James,* Viking Press, New York, 1967.

Ames, James Barr: "Harvard University," in Charles F. Richardson and Henry A. Clark (eds.), *The College Book,* Osgood & Co., Boston, 1878.

Ames, James Barr: "Lawrence Scientific School," in Charles F. Richardson and Henry A. Clark (eds.), *The College Book,* Osgood & Co., Boston, 1878.

Angell, James B.: *The Higher Education: A Plea for Making It Accessible to All,* Board of Regents, Ann Arbor, Mich., 1879.

Angell, Robert C.: *The Campus,* D. Appleton & Co., Inc., New York, 1928.

Aurner, Clarence Ray: *History of Education in Iowa,* vol. IV, State Historical Society of Iowa, Iowa City, 1916.

Aydelotte, Frank: *Breaking the Academic Lock Step: The Development of Honors Work in American Colleges and Universities,* Harper & Brothers, New York, 1944.

Bagg, Lyman H.: *Four Years at Yale,* C. C. Chatfield & Co., New Haven, Conn., 1871.

Bailyn, Bernard: *Education in the Forming of American Society,* University of North Carolina Press, Chapel Hill, 1960.

Baldwin, Bird T.: *Present Status of the Honor System in Colleges and Universities,* Government Printing Office, Washington, D.C., 1915.

**Barnard, Frederick A. P.:** *Analysis of Some Statistics of Collegiate Education,* printed for the use of the trustees, Columbia University, New York, 1870.

**Battle, Kemp P.:** *History of the University of North Carolina,* vol. I, Edwards & Broughton Printing Co., Raleigh, N.C., 1907–1912.

**Bealle, Morris A.:** *The History of Football at Harvard, 1874–1948,* Columbia Publishing Co., Washington, D.C., 1948.

**Benn, John A.:** *Columbus—Undergraduate,* J. B. Lippincott Company, Philadelphia, 1928.

**Berelson, Bernard:** *Graduate Education in the United States,* McGraw-Hill Book Company, New York, 1960.

**Bishop, Morris:** *A History of Cornell,* Cornell University Press, Ithaca, N.Y., 1962.

**Blackorby, Edward C.:** *Prairie Rebel,* University of Nebraska Press, Lincoln, 1963.

**Bowman, Claude C.:** *The College Professor in America,* University of Pennsylvania Press, Philadelphia, 1938.

**Brocklesby, William C.:** "Trinity College," in Charles F. Richardson and Henry Clark (eds.), *The College Book,* Osgood & Co., Boston, 1878.

**Broderick, Francis:** *DuBois,* Stanford University Press, Stanford, Calif., 1959.

**Bronson, Walter C.:** *The History of Brown University 1764–1914,* Brown University, Providence, R.I., 1914.

**Broome, Edwin C.:** *A Historical and Critical Discussion of College Admission Requirements,* The Macmillan Company, New York, 1903.

**Brown, Kenneth I.:** *A Campus Decade: The Hiram Study Plan of Intensive Courses,* University of Chicago Press, Chicago, 1940.

**Brubacher, John S., and Willis Rudy:** *Higher Education in Transition,* Harper & Brothers, New York, 1958.

**Bruce, Philip A.:** *History of the University of Virginia 1819–1919,* 2 vols., The Macmillan Company, New York, 1920.

**Buckley, William:** *God and Man at Yale,* Henry Regnery Company, Chicago, 1951.

**Bullock, Henry A.:** *A History of Negro Education in the South from 1619 to the Present,* Harvard University Press, Cambridge, Mass., 1967.

**Bureau of the Census:** *Historical Statistics of the United States,* Washington, D.C., 1957.

**Burgess, John W.:** *The American University: When Shall It Be? Where Shall It Be? What Shall It Be?,* Ginn, Heath & Co., Boston, 1884.

**Bush, George G.:** *History of Higher Education in Massachusetts,* Government Printing Office, Washington, D.C., 1891.

**Buster, Josephine M.:** "Which College—White or Negro?" *The Crisis,* **10** (1933).

**Caliver, Ambrose:** "Some Tendencies in Higher Education and Their Application to the Negro College," *Opportunity,* **6**:6ff. (1928).

**Callcott, George H.:** *A History of the University of Maryland,* Maryland Historical Society, Baltimore, 1966.

**Campbell, Thomas M.:** *The Moveable School Goes to the Negro Farmer,* Tuskegee Institute Press, Tuskegee, Ala., 1936.

**Canby, Henry Seidel:** *College Sons and College Fathers,* Harper & Brothers, New York, 1915.

**Candler, A. D.** (ed.): *Colonial Records of Georgia,* vol. XIX, Part II, Franklin Printing & Publishing Co., Atlanta, 1911.

**Canfield, James H.:** *The College Student and His Problems,* The Macmillan Company, New York, 1902.

**Caplow, Theodore, and Reece J. McGee:** *The Academic Marketplace,* Basic Books, Inc., Publishers, New York, 1959.

*Catalogue of the Officers and Students of the College of New Jersey for 1844–1846,* Princeton University, Princeton, N.J., 1846.

**Chambers, William N.:** *Old Bullion Benton Senator from the West,* Little, Brown & Company, Boston, 1956.

**Chessman, G. Wallace:** *Denison: The Story of an Ohio College,* Denison University, Granville, Ohio, 1957.

**Cheyney, Edward P.:** *History of the University of Pennsylvania 1740–1940,* University of Pennsylvania Press, Philadelphia, 1940.

**Christensen, J. C.:** *University Business Administration,* Kansas Agricultural College, Topeka, 1912.

**Churchman, Philip H.:** "The Sliding Scale and Academic Standards," *Educational Review,* vol. 27, June, 1912.

**Clark, Willis G.:** "History of Education in Alabama 1702–1889," in Herbert V. Adams (ed.), *Contributions to American Educational History,* Government Printing Office, Washington, D.C., 1889.

**Cobban, Alan B.:** *The King's Hall within the University of Cambridge,* Cambridge University Press, Cambridge, 1969.

**Collins, Varnum L.:** *Princeton,* Oxford University Press, New York, 1914.

**Cometti, Elizabeth** (ed.): *Seeing America and Its Great Men: The Journal and Letters of Count Francesco del Verme 1783–1784,* University of Virginia Press, Charlottesville, 1969.

Cooper, Clayton S.: *Why Go to College,* The Century Co., New York, 1912.

Cowley, W. H.: "The History of Student Residential Housing," *School and Society,* **40** (1934).

Crane, R. T.: *The Utility of All Kinds of Higher Schooling,* H. O. Shepard Co., Chicago, 1909.

Cross, Robert D.: *The Emergence of Liberal Catholicism in America,* Harvard University Press, Cambridge, Mass., 1958.

Curti, Merle, and Vernon Carstensen: *The University of Wisconsin: a History 1848–1925,* vol. I, University of Wisconsin Press, Madison, 1949.

Cutler, W. P., and J. P. (eds.): *Life, Journals, and Correspondence of Reverend Manasseh Cutler,* vol. II, R. Clarke & Co., Cincinnati, Ohio, 1888.

Cutting, George R.: *Student Life at Amherst,* Hatch & Williams, Amherst, Mass., 1871.

Dartmouth College Senior Committee: *The Report on Undergraduate Education,* Part 1, Hanover, N.H., 1924.

Doolittle, R. S.: "Rutgers College," in Charles F. Richardson and Henry A. Clark (eds.), *The College Book,* Osgood & Co., Boston, 1878.

DuBois, W. E. B.: "The Negro College," *The Crisis,* **40** (1933).

Durfee, Calvin: *A History of Williams College,* A. Williams & Co., Boston, 1860.

Dyer, John P.: *Tulane: The Biography of a University, 1834–1965,* Harper & Row, Publishers, Incorporated, New York, 1966.

Easterby, James H.: *History of the College of Charleston Founded 1770,* College of Charleston, Charleston, S.C., 1935.

Eddy, Edward D.: *Colleges for Our Land and Time; the Land-Grant Idea in American Education,* Harper & Brothers, New York, 1957.

Eells, Walter C.: *Baccalaureate Degrees Conferred by American Colleges in the 17th and 18th Centuries,* Washington, D.C., 1958.

Eliot, Charles W.: "The Cultivated Man," National Education Association, *Journal of Proceedings and Addresses,* Winona, Minn., 1903.

Eliot, Charles W.: *University Administration,* Houghton Mifflin Company, Boston, 1908.

Eliot, Charles W.: "Wherein Public Education Has Failed," *Forum,* vol. 14, 1892.

Erbacher, Sebastian A.: *Catholic Higher Education for Men in the United States, 1850–1866,* Catholic University of America, Washington, D.C., 1931.

**Evans, Medford Stanton:** *Revolt on the Campus,* Henry Regnery Company, Chicago, 1961.

**Fairchild, James H.:** "Oberlin College," in Charles F. Richardson and Henry A. Clark (eds.), *The College Book,* Osgood & Co., Boston, 1878.

**Feuer, Lewis S.:** *The Conflict of Generations,* Basic Books, Inc., New York, 1969.

**Fisher, Dorothy Canfield:** *The Bent Twig,* Henry Holt and Company, Inc., New York, 1915.

**Fisher, Sydney G.:** *American Education,* R. G. Badger, Boston, 1917.

**Flandrau, Charles M.:** *Harvard Episodes,* Copeland & Day, Boston, 1897.

**Fleming, Walter L.:** *Louisiana State University 1860–1896,* Louisiana State University Press, Baton Rouge, 1936.

**Fletcher, Robert S.:** *A History of Oberlin College,* vol. I, Oberlin College, Oberlin, Ohio, 1943.

**Flipper, Henry O.:** *A Colored Cadet at West Point,* H. Lee & Co., New York, 1878.

**Freidel, Frank B.:** *Franklin D. Roosevelt: The Apprenticeship,* Little, Brown and Company, Boston, 1952.

**Fuess, Claude M.:** *The College Board: Its First Fifty Years,* Columbia University Press, New York, 1950.

**Gavit, John Palmer:** *College,* Harcourt, Brace & World, Inc., New York, 1925.

**Geiger, Louis G.:** *University of the Northern Plains: A History of North Dakota,* North Dakota University Press, Grand Forks, 1958.

**Gilman, Daniel C.:** *The Benefits Which Society Derives from Universities,* The Johns Hopkins Press, Baltimore, 1885.

**Gilman, Daniel C.:** *The Building of the University: An Inaugural Address Delivered at Oakland, Nov. 7th, 1872,* J. H. Carmany & Company, San Francisco, 1872.

"Glimpses of Old College Life," *William and Mary Quarterly,* vol. 7, 1900.

**Godbold, Albea:** *The Church College of the Old South,* Duke University Press, Durham, N.C., 1962.

**Goodstein, Anita S.:** *Biography of a Businessman: Henry W. Sage 1814–1896,* Cornell University Press, Ithaca, N.Y., 1962.

"The Great Rebellion at Princeton," *William and Mary Quarterly,* vol. 16, 1907.

**Hadley, Arthur T.:** "Wealth and Democracy in American Colleges," *Harper's New Monthly Magazine,* **113** (1906).

Hadley, Arthur T. (ed.): "Yale University," *Four American Universities,* Harper & Brothers, New York, 1895.

Hall, G. Stanley: *Life and Confessions of a Psychologist,* D. Appleton & Company, Inc., New York, 1923.

Hall, G. Stanley: "Student Customs," *Proceedings for October 1900,* American Antiquarian Society, vol. 14, part I, Worcester, Mass., 1901.

Handlin, Oscar: "Are the Colleges Killing Education?" *Atlantic Monthly,* 209:41ff. (1962).

Handlin, Oscar: *John Dewey's Challenge to Education,* Harper & Brothers, New York, 1959.

Handlin, Oscar: "Yearning for Security," *Atlantic Monthly,* 187:25ff. (1951).

Handlin, Oscar and Mary F.: *The Dimensions of Liberty,* Harvard University Press, Cambridge, Mass., 1961.

Handlin, Oscar and Mary F.: "Ethnic Factors and Social Mobility," *Explorations in Entrepreneurial History,* 9:1–7 (1956).

Harper, William Rainey: *The Trend in Higher Education,* University of Chicago Press, Chicago, 1905.

Harris, Seymour E.: *The Market for College Graduates,* Harvard University Press, Cambridge, Mass., 1949.

Harvard University, Committee on the Objectives of a General Education in a Free Society: *General Education in a Free Society,* Report of the Harvard committee, with an introduction by James B. Conant, Harvard University Press, Cambridge, Mass., 1945.

Hatch, Louis C.: *The History of Bowdoin College,* Shorter & Harmar, Portland, Maine, 1927.

Havighurst, Walter: *The Miami Years 1809–1959,* G. P. Putnam's Sons, New York, 1958.

Henderson, Algo D., and Dorothy Hall: *Antioch College: Its Design for Liberal Education,* Harper & Brothers, New York, 1946.

Henderson, Joseph L.: *Admission to College by Certificate,* Teachers College, Columbia University, New York, 1912.

Hergesheimer, Joseph: *Cytherea,* Alfred A. Knopf, Inc., New York, 1922.

Hitchcock, Edward: *Reminiscences of Amherst College,* Bridgman & Childs, Northampton, Mass., 1863.

Hofstadter, Richard, and C. Dewitt Hardy: *The Development and Scope of Higher Education in the United States,* Columbia University Press, New York, 1952.

Hollis, Daniel: *University of South Carolina,* vol. I, University of South Carolina Press, Columbia, 1951–1956.

Holmes, Dwight O. H.: *The Evolution of the Negro College,* Teachers College, Columbia University, New York, 1934.

Hoover, Thomas N.: *The History of Ohio University,* Ohio University Press, Athens, 1954.

Hughes, Langston: "Cowards from the College," *The Crisis,* **40–41:**226 (August, 1934).

Hutchins, Robert Maynard: *The Higher Learning in America,* Yale University Press, New Haven, Conn., 1936.

James, William: "The Ph.D. Octopus," *Harvard Monthly,* **36:**1–9 (1903).

Jastrow, Joseph: "The Administrative Peril in Education," *Popular Science Monthly,* November, 1912.

Johnson, Edward, in J. F. Jameson (ed.): *Wonder-Working Providence 1628–1651,* Charles Scribner's Sons, New York, 1910.

Jones, Barbara: *Bennington College: The Development of an Educational Idea,* Harper & Brothers, New York, 1946.

Kelly, Maurice: "Professeur," *American Mercury,* **8:**16 (1926).

Keppel, Frederick P.: *The Foundation: Its Place in American Life,* The Macmillan Company, New York, 1930.

Kingsley, William L.: "Yale College," in Charles F. Richardson and Henry A. Clark (eds.), *The College Book,* Osgood & Co., Boston, 1878.

Kinsey, Alfred C.: *Sexual Behavior in the Human Female,* W. B. Saunders Company, Philadelphia, 1953.

Kinsey, Alfred C.: *Sexual Behavior in the Human Male,* W. B. Saunders Company, Philadelphia, 1948.

Kirkpatrick, J. E.: *The American College and Its Rulers,* New Republic, Inc., New York, 1926.

Lazarsfeld, Paul F., and Wagner Thielens, Jr.: *The Academic Mind: Social Scientists in a Time of Crisis,* The Free Press, Glencoe, Ill., 1958.

LeDuc, Thomas: *Piety and Intellect at Amherst College 1865–1912,* Columbia University Press, New York, 1946.

March, F. A.: "Lafayette College," in Charles F. Richardson and Henry A. Clark (eds.), *The College Book,* Osgood & Co., Boston, 1878.

Matthews, Brander: "Columbia University," in Arthur Hadley (ed.), *Four American Universities,* Harper & Brothers, New York, 1895.

McAnear, Beverly: "College Founding in the American Colonies, 1745–1775," *Mississippi Valley Historical Review,* **42:**24ff. (1955).

McCarthy, Charles: *The Wisconsin Idea,* The Macmillan Company, New York, 1912.

McCosh, James: "Discipline in American Colleges," *North American Review,* vol. 262, 1878.

McGrath, Earl J.: *The Evolution of Administrative Offices in Institutions of Higher Education in the United States from 1860 to 1933,* University of Chicago Library, Chicago, 1938.

McMillan, Lewis K.: *Negro Higher Education in the State of South Carolina,* South Carolina State College, Orangeburg, 1952.

Meiklejohn, Alexander: *The Experimental College,* University of Wisconsin Press, Madison, 1928.

Meriwether, Colyer: *History of Education in South Carolina,* Government Printing Office, Washington, D.C., 1889.

Millis, William A.: *The History of Hanover College from 1827 to 1927,* Hanover College, Hanover, Ind., 1927.

Mims, Edwin: *History of Vanderbilt University,* Vanderbilt University, Nashville, Tenn., 1946.

Miner, Dwight C. (ed.): *A History of Columbia College on Morningside,* Columbia University Press, New York, 1954.

Montross, Lynn and Lois S.: *Town and Gown,* George H. Doran and Company, New York, 1923.

Morgan, James Henry: *Dickinson College: The History of One Hundred and Fifty Years 1783–1933,* Dickinson College, Carlisle, Pa., 1933.

Morison, Samuel Eliot: *The Founding of Harvard College,* Harvard University Press, Cambridge, Mass., 1935.

Morison, Samuel Eliot: *Harvard College in the Seventeenth Century,* 2 vols., Harvard University Press, Cambridge, Mass., 1936.

Morison, Samuel Eliot: *Three Centuries of Harvard, 1636–1936,* Harvard University Press, Cambridge, Mass., 1936.

Nation, Carry A.: *The Use and Need of the Life of Carry A. Nation,* F. M. Steves, Sons, Topeka, Kans., 1909.

*New England's First Fruits,* London, 1643.

*New York Times,* Jan. 12, 1923.

Norton, Charles E.: "Harvard University," in Arthur Hadley (ed.), *Four American Universities,* Harper & Brothers, New York, 1895.

Notestein, Lucy L.: *Wooster of the Middle West,* Yale University Press, New Haven, Conn., 1937.

"Original Papers in Relation to a Course of Liberal Education," *American Journal of Science and Arts,* vol. 15, 1829.

Packard, G. T.: "Bowdoin College," in Charles F. Richardson and Henry A. Clark (eds.), *The College Book,* Osgood & Co., Boston, 1878.

Palmer, Alice Freeman, quoted in Waitman Barbe: *Going to College with the Opinions of Fifty Leading College Presidents and Educators,* Earhart & Richardson, Cincinnati, Ohio, 1899.

Paton, Stewart: "American Monarchies," *The Evening Post,* New York, Feb. 11, 1911.

Patton, John: *Jefferson, Cabell and the University of Virginia,* Neale Publishing Co., New York, 1906.

Perry, Charles M.: *Henry Philip Tappan,* University of Michigan Press, Ann Arbor, 1933.

Pierson, George W.: *Yale College: An Educational History 1871–1937,* vol. 1, Yale University Press, New Haven, Conn., 1952.

Pomfret, John E.: "Student Interests at Brown 1789–1790," *New England Quarterly,* 5 (1932).

Porter, Noah: *The American Colleges and the American Public,* C. C. Chatfield & Co., New Haven, Conn., 1870.

Power, Edward J.: *A History of Catholic Higher Education in the United States,* Bruce Publishing Company, Milwaukee, 1958.

President's Commission on Higher Education: *Higher Education for American Democracy,* a report, I, II, III, IV, V, Washington, D.C., 1947.

*Publishers' Weekly,* Sept. 15, 1969.

Quincy, Josiah: *The History of Harvard University,* 2 vols., J. Owen, Cambridge, Mass., 1840.

Rammelkamp, Charles H.: *Illinois College: A Centennial History 1829–1929,* Yale University Press, New Haven, Conn., 1928.

Raymond, Andrew Van V.: *Union University,* vol. 1, Lewis Publishing Co., New York, 1907.

Richardson, Charles F., and Henry A. Clark (eds.): *The College Book,* Osgood & Co., Boston, 1878.

Richardson, Charles F., and Henry A. Clark: "Military Academy," *The College Book,* Osgood & Co., Boston, 1878.

Richardson, Charles F., and Henry A. Clark: "Naval Academy," *The College Book,* Osgood & Co., Boston, 1878.

Richardson, J. D. (ed.): *Messages and Papers of the Presidents,* Government Printing Office, Washington, D.C., 1896.

Rogers, Walter P.: *Andrew D. White and the Modern University,* Cornell University Press, Ithaca, N.Y., 1942.

Rosenberger, Jesse L.: *Rochester, the Making of a University,* University of Rochester, Rochester, N.Y., 1927.

Ross, Earle D.: *Democracy's College: The Land-grant Movement in the Formative State,* Iowa State College Press, Ames, 1942.

Rudolph, Frederick: *The American College and University,* Alfred A. Knopf, Inc., New York, 1962.

Rudolph, Frederick: *Mark Hopkins and the Log: Williams College, 1836–1872,* Yale University Press, New Haven, Conn., 1956.

Ryan, W. Carson, Jr., (ed.): *Studies in Early Graduate Education,* Carnegie Foundation for the Advancement of Teaching, New York, 1939.

Ryan, W. Carson, Jr.: *The Literature of American School and College Athletics,* Carnegie Foundation for the Advancement of Teaching, New York, 1929.

Sanford, Nevitt (ed.): *The American College: A Psychological and Social Interpretation of Higher Learning,* John Wiley & Sons, Inc., New York, 1962.

Santayana, George: *Character and Opinion in the United States,* W. W. Norton & Company, Inc., New York, 1934.

Schmidt, George P.: *The Old Time College President,* Columbia University Press, New York, 1930.

Sears, Jesse B.: *Philanthropy in the History of American Higher Education,* Government Printing Office, Washington, D.C., 1922.

Shedd, Clarence P.: *Two Centuries of Student Christian Movements, Their Origins and Intercollegiate Life,* Association Press, New York, 1934.

Shipton, Clifford K.: "Ye Mystery of Ye Ages Solved or, How Placing Worked at Colonial Harvard and Yale," *Harvard Alumni Bulletin,* vol. 57, 1954.

Sims, J. Marion: *The Story of My Life,* D. Appleton & Company, Inc., New York, 1885.

Sinclair, Upton: *The Goose-Step: A Study of American Education,* Albert & Charles Boni, Inc., New York, 1922.

Sloane, William M.: "Princeton University," in Arthur Hadley (ed.), *Four American Universities,* Harper & Brothers, New York, 1895.

Slosson, Edwin E.: *Great American Universities,* The Macmillan Company, New York, 1910.

**Smythe, George F.:** *Kenyon College: Its First Century,* Yale University Press, New Haven, Conn., 1924.

**Snow, Louis F.:** *The College Curriculum in the United States,* privately printed, New York, 1907.

**Spafford, Ivol et al.:** *Building a Curriculum for General Education: A Psychological and Social Interpretation of Higher Learning,* University of Minnesota, Minneapolis, 1943.

**Stillé, C. J.:** "University of Pennsylvania," in Charles F. Richardson and Henry A. Clark (eds.), *The College Book,* Osgood & Co., Boston, 1878.

**Storr, Richard J.:** *Harper's University: The Beginnings,* University of Chicago Press, Chicago, 1966.

**Sweet, William W.:** *Indiana Asbury-DePauw University, 1837–1937,* Abingdon Press, New York, 1937.

**Tappan, Henry P.:** *University Education,* G. P. Putnam's Sons, New York, 1951.

**Tewksbury, Donald G.:** *The Founding of American Colleges and Universities before the Civil War,* Teachers College, Columbia University, New York, 1932.

**Thwing, Charles F.:** *A History of Higher Education in America,* D. Appleton & Company, Inc., New York, 1906.

**Ticknor, George:** *Remarks on Changes Lately Proposed or Adopted in Harvard University,* Cummings, Hilliard & Co., Boston, 1825.

**Tocqueville, Alexis de:** *Democracy in America,* 2 vols., Alfred A. Knopf, Inc., New York, 1944.

**True, Alfred D.:** *A History of Agricultural Extension Work in the United States, 1785–1923,* Government Printing Office, Washington, D.C., 1928.

**United States Office of Education:** *Education Directory 1960–1961,* Washington, D.C., 1960.

**Van Amringe, John H. et al.:** *History of Columbia University 1754–1904,* Columbia University Press, New York, 1904.

**Veblen, Thorstein:** *The Higher Learning in America,* Hill & Wang, Inc., New York, 1965.

**Viles, Jonas:** *The University of Missouri: A Centennial History,* University of Missouri Press, Columbia, 1939.

**Vinton, Frederick:** "The College of New Jersey," in Charles F. Richardson and Henry A. Clark (eds.), *The College Book,* Osgood & Co., Boston, 1878.

Wayland, Francis: *Elements of Political Economy,* Leavitt, Lord & Co., New York, 1837.

Wayland, Francis: *Thoughts on the Present Collegiate System in the United States,* Gould, Kendall & Lincoln, Boston, 1842.

Wayland, Francis and H. L.: *A Memoir of the Life and Labors of Francis Wayland,* 2 vols., Sheldon & Co., New York, 1867.

Wechsler, James: *Revolt on Campus,* Covici, Friede, Inc., New York, 1935.

Wells, William: "Union College," in Charles F. Richardson and Henry A. Clark (eds.), *The College Book,* Osgood & Co., Boston, 1878.

Wertenbaker, Thomas J.: *Princeton 1746–1896,* Princeton University Press, Princeton, 1946.

Whalen, Richard J. : *The Founding Father,* New American Library, Inc. , New York, 1964.

White, Andrew D.: *A History of the Warfare of Science with Theology,* vol. 1, D. Appleton & Company, Inc., New York, 1896.

Wilson, Logan: *The Academic Man,* Oxford University Press, New York, 1942.

Winchester, C. R.: "Wesleyan University," in Charles F. Richardson and Henry A. Clark (eds.), *The College Book,* Osgood & Co., Boston, 1878.

Wister, Owen: *Philosophy 4: A Story of Harvard University,* The Macmillan Company, New York, 1903.

Woodward, William H.: *Studies in Education during the Age of the Renaissance 1400–1600,* Teachers College Classics in Education No. 32, Teachers College Press, Columbia University, New York, 1967.

Woody, Thomas: *Quaker Education in the Colony and State of New Jersey,* privately printed, Philadelphia, 1923.

# *Index*